SEXUAL BARGAINING
Power Politics in the American Marriage

JOHN SCANZONI

is Associate Professor of Sociology at Indiana University. He is the author of *Opportunity and the Family* and *The Black Family in Modern Society* as well as articles in various sociological reviews, and is a former Deputy Editor of *American Sociological Review*.

SEXUAL
BARGAINING

Power Politics
in the
American Marriage

JOHN SCANZONI

A SPECTRUM BOOK

PRENTICE-HALL, INC. ENGLEWOOD CLIFFS, N.J.

Library of Congress Cataloging in Publication Data

Scanzoni, John H   1935–
    Sexual bargaining.

    (A Spectrum book)
    Bibliography: p. 165
    1. Marriage—U. S.   2. Husband and wife—U. S.
3. Sex roles. I. Title.
HQ536.S35   301.42   71–39749
ISBN   0–13–807461–5
ISBN   0–13–807453–4 (pbk.)

Material from Peter M. Blau, *Exchange and Power in Social Life* (copyright © 1964 by John Wiley & Sons, Inc.) is reprinted by kind permission of the publisher.

Material from John Scanzoni, *Opportunity and the Family* (copyright © 1970 by The Macmillan Company) is reprinted by kind permission of the publisher.

10   9   8   7   6   5   4   3   2   1

Prentice-Hall International, Inc. (*London*)
Prentice-Hall of Australia Pty. Ltd. (*Sydney*)
Prentice-Hall of Canada Ltd. (*Toronto*)
Prentice-Hall of India Private Limited (*New Delhi*)
Prentice-Hall of Japan, Inc. (*Tokyo*)

Contents

Preface

This book was initially undertaken in the fall of 1969 at the suggestion of J. Richard Udry. The author is indebted both to Professor Udry and to Professor William J. Goode for their careful reading and constructive criticisms of an earlier version of the manuscript. Thanks are also due to Mike Hunter and Marjorie Streeter of Prentice-Hall for their confidence in the manuscript and their help in bringing it to fruition. To my wife Letha I am indebted for practical instruction on how pleasant it can be to live with a liberated woman.

In many respects, the contents of the book are a response to issues raised by students and colleagues in connection with two earlier volumes by the author. As such it represents one phase of a continuing dialogue surrounding important issues. The non-sociology undergraduate student and layman should find the following discussion understandable and useful both in personal and public policy terms. At the same time the professional sociologist and graduate and undergraduate sociology students should find the theoretical perspective provocative enough to continue the dialogue already begun, and perhaps to undertake further research to determine the extent of its validity.

SEXUAL BARGAINING
Power Politics in the American Marriage

Introduction

There are several questions about contemporary marriage patterns that this book can help answer. First, many people are asking "Is marriage breaking down?" They hear reports of alleged catastrophic divorce rates and believe the answer is "yes." Second, some younger people are asking "Is marriage as we have known it largely irrelevant? Do alleged widespread sexual experimentation, the pill, communal living, and group marriage render the conjugal, monogamous relationship an historical anachronism?" Third, professionals in the social and behavioral sciences are asking whether present forms of marriage are changing, and if so, into what, and how rapidly? Finally, a question being asked by students, laymen, and professionals alike is "How extensive is the current 'revolution' in women's roles, and how does it connect with questions of family 'breakdown,' 'irrelevancy,' and 'change'?" We shall try to deal with all four questions because they are intimately related, though as we shall see, the first two are spurious. Modern marriage is neither collapsing nor passé. Change there indeed is, and a great deal of it, both historical and current, is linked to male-female sex roles and to the potential for conflict between them.

PLAN OF THE BOOK

Chapter one, "The Myth of Marital Disintegration," deals with the alleged breakdown of modern marriage. It describes where we are right now in terms of divorce trends both in the United States and in other developed nations. It sets the tone for the remainder of the book because it assumes that to assess trends within contemporary marital structure we need be neither Pollyanna nor naïve, neither hysterical nor sensational.

Chapter two, "Marriage in the Process of Change," puts the present marital structure in historical perspective. It endeavors to explain some of the reasons for divorce trends described in chapter one. This chapter also takes up the origins of women's liberation in the early 1800s and traces it to the present time. Changes in marital structure that have occured throughout this era are discussed and linked to the rise of feminism.

Chapter three, "The Motivation to Marry" looks at some of the ways males and females currently learn their respective sex roles, and how these socialization patterns influence love relationships prior to marriage, as well as marriage decisions themselves. The idea of male-female exchange, or reciprocity, is introduced here, along with the idea that reward-seeking is the basis for the formation of premarital and marital arrangements.

Chapter four, "Marital Conflict as a Positive Force," builds on the ideas of male-female exchanges and reward-seeking. We show how contemporary marriages are held together through social exchange, how these exchanges may develop into husband-wife conflict, and how conflict may lead either to divorce or to *changes* in marriage, including changes which point toward the emergence of future marriage forms.

Having built up to chapter five, "The Future of Marriage," we are ready for a close look at those trends and changes that might influence future patterns of marriage and the family. We talk about those family "experiments" such as communes and group marriages that do not make equality between the sexes an explicit factor. We look at the relationships of Neofeminism, or Women's Liberation, to other liberation movements, including the black movement. Considerable attention is given to that emerging form of marriage which is genuinely new, but which at the same time has its roots in the historical events and current circumstances described in the preceding chapters.

THEME OF THE BOOK

The central theme of the book is that of reward-seeking between males and females, which in turn generates social exchanges between them, which in turn generate conflicts and changes. We want to make quite explicit the place and outcome of conflict within marriage, both historically and currently. Our focus will be solely on husband-wife (not parent-child or kin-family) conflict. In many past discussions of marriage, the theme of conflict has often been ignored or else treated as a negative force. We shall attempt to show that conflict is an intrinsic part of marriage (as it is to any social system) and also that it may have positive as well as negative consequences.

Specifically, we shall look at the husband-wife relationship as a set of roles. Historically, the male role has been dominant, the female role subordinate. Over the last 170 years wives have sought greater rewards from marriage, including less subordination to husbands, by means of exchange, bargaining, and conflict. Husbands have, over the period, reluctantly relinquished many rights and privileges, though they still remain dominant. Female reward-seeking has thus produced change, and one unintended byproduct of these changes has been gradual increases in the rates of marital dissolution.

Present and future changes in marriage forms and in sex roles are basically a continuation of these long-term conflicts between males and females. The publicity given to the revival of American Feminism has made people of all groups and ages aware as never before of the demands (reward-seeking) of some women. The trend of the future may very well be that as some of the counterproductive tactics of some Women's Liberation groups give way to more rational action, more and more younger women will come to want sex-role equality both within marriage as well as out of it—for unless there is actual equality in both spheres, there cannot be full equality in either. The inexorable trend toward equality, and all the things associated with it, will certainly continue to have consequences for the future of marriage. In these pages, therefore, we shall try to capture and combine past, present, and future aspects of marital structure and process—all within the framework of male-female reward-seeking, reciprocity, and conflict.

1. The Myth of Marital Disintegration

"The family has fallen apart. Nearly half of all marriages end in divorce." [1]

Our purpose in this chapter is to examine official government data to see, first of all, just how much accuracy there is to such oft-made assertions as the one above. Second, we want to see how correct the assertion is that allaged high divorce rates indicate that marriage, as we know it, is in a state of disintegration. The position we shall take is that divorce data have been misused and abused, and that a careful reading of them does not support the idea of widespread marital disintegration.

> One analyst has predicted that one-third to one-half of all marriages occurring this year are destined to end in a divorce court. [2]

No reference is made, however, to the identity of the "analyst," nor to where the analyst got his information. One suspects that there is a circle of "analysts" who quote each other on divorce statistics, and whose quotes are in turn disseminated to millions of people through the media, but that no one (including the experts) bothers to check the validity of anyone else's sources.

It is essential that we start with as accurate and as undistorted a picture as possible of current levels of marital stability in the United States and in other modern nations. In subsequent chapters we will examine some historic and current factors that help to account for present trends in marital patterns. Finally, with an accurate picture of marriage now and in the past established, we will be in a good position to make responsible projections about its *future*.

1. Dunbar, p. 487.
2. Otto, p. 1.

In considering the future of marriage, it makes considerable difference if, on the one hand, we accept the notion that there is a vast, headlong rush to the divorce courts, that large numbers of persons can hardly wait to divorce their present mate and marry the next, and that this shows that the present system is so bad that something radically different must be taking its place; or if, on the other hand, one questions the misuse of divorce data and holds that current divorce behavior signals not so much a rejection of the marriage system per se, but instead an unwillingness to tolerate unsatisfactory experiences within the system. Those who hold the first view might predict rather convulsive changes in marriage within the foreseeable future. Those who hold the second might predict, for the vast bulk of the population, continuation of the long-term *evolution* in marital structure that has been in motion for almost two hundred years. The second is the position taken here. It seems clear that while genuine change in marital structure is in the offing, it is not cataclysmic, but instead will gradually grow out of present marital patterns.

DISSOLUTION RATES IN THE UNITED STATES

LIMITATIONS OF CENSUS DATA

Unfortunately, as with almost all social science data, even the best statistics on marriage and divorce are subject to many kinds of random and systematic error.[3] Besides the limitations of statistics there is the additional problem of definition. There is a "final decree of absolute divorce" which permits remarriage, and there is also the "limited decree of divorce" (legal separation) which does not.[4] Then there is the "annulment of marriage" in which the court decrees that a "valid marriage" has never taken place at all. In the United States official divorce statistics combine annulments with absolute decrees. ("Annulments account for only about 3 percent of the combined total.")[5] Sometimes, both in the United States and in other countries, limited decrees are counted in the total by mistake.

A related problem arises from the increasingly liberalized allowance of absolute decrees. In countries such as England and in many of the fifty states, absolute divorce was granted, until recently, only on grounds of proven adultery. As laws become increasingly more "permissive," divorce rates rise as a result of legal, not of newly erupting social or psychological factors. Take the legal fees of a divorce. Poorer people may

---

3. *See* Carter and Glick, 1970, for a thorough discussion of the subject.
4. *Ibid.*, pp. 26–27.
5. *Ibid.*, p. 54.

not be able to afford the fees, so they either desert, separate, or simply stay together because there seems "no way out." But early in 1971 the U.S. Supreme Court ruled that no one can be denied divorce simply because he cannot afford the legal costs. Consequently, many poorer people may suddenly seek divorce owing to this ruling. Thus divorce rates may rise sharply for a time, but the reasons for this *particular* rise are not directly related to any new trends or attitudes about marriage.

CRUDE DIVORCE RATES

"Divorces have increased greatly in the United States, as is well known," wrote Groves and Ogburn in 1928.[6] Figure 1.1 indicates that the trend

FIG. 1.1 DIVORCE RATES: UNITED STATES, 1920–67

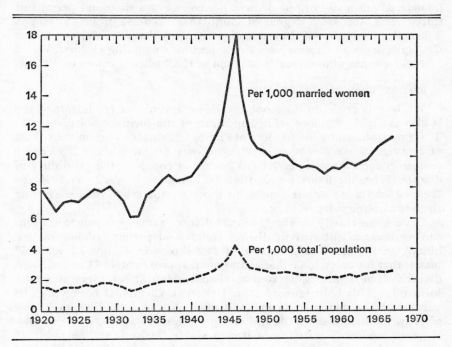

SOURCE: Plateris, December, 1970.

they observed (begun in the 1860s) has continued up to the present time. The "crude divorce rate" (lower line in the figure) represents the number

6. Groves and Ogburn, 1928, p. 346.

of divorces per 1,000 persons. In 1969, for instance, for every cohort of 1,000 men, women, and children, there were estimated to be 3.3 divorces, or just about three for every thousand Americans. The trend since 1860 can be summarized as follows: from 1860 to shortly after 1910 the crude divorce rate rose steadily but remained below 1.0. After an additional thirty years (1940), the crude rate became 2.0 though there was a substantial drop in the rate during the worst years of the Great Depression (1930–33). In six more years (1946) the crude rate jumped to 4.3 (the highest figure ever in our nation's history), but this was attributed to the massive upheavals and "quickie marriages" of World War II. From 1947 to 1958, the United States experienced a steady decline in the crude divorce rate to about where it was prior to the war. Since then it has resumed its long-term gradual increase to the current figure of approximately 3.0, or a rise of one divorce per cohort of a thousand persons in thirty years, the same degree of climb that occurred from 1910–1940. The major limitation of the crude divorce rate is that the cohort on which the figure is based encompasses single persons (including children under fifteen)—people who obviously are "not at risk" when it comes to divorce.

REFINED DIVORCE RATES

While this criticism does not invalidate use of the crude rate, there is also available a "more refined measure of the incidence of divorce." [7] This rate is shown by the top line of Figure 1.1, and is based on the cohort of every *1,000 married women* who are over fifteen years of age. Every person in such a cohort is "at risk" when it comes to the possibility of divorce. From the figure we see that the long-term upward trends in the "refined" divorce rate are similar to those for the crude rate, suggesting the latter's basic validity.

If we focus chiefly on the "refined" divorce rate, what generalizations can we make about current divorce trends and patterns of marital stability? On the one hand, the rate of 11.2 shown in Figure 1.1 for 1967 means that for every 1,000 married women, approximately 11 experienced divorce. (The figure is, of course, almost identical for every thousand husbands.) This is little more than 1 percent. Clearly, if better than 98 percent of the married women (and men) do not seek divorces in any given year, there seems little indication of *mass* dissatisfaction with marriage, or *wholesale rejection* of it as a viable institution. The publicity given to Hollywood divorces and the misuse by some of certain kinds of divorce statistics combine to distort the actual stability of the great majority of American marriages.

On the other hand, Figure 1.1 shows definite increases over time in both

7. Plateris, 1967, p. 3.

types of divorce rates. Plateris claims "that the recent increases in the number and rates of divorce are not due exclusively to changes in the population, but are also, at least in part, due to a higher likelihood of the occurrence of divorce." [8] Increases in divorce cannot be explained solely by an increased population. Married persons are in fact more likely to obtain divorces now than they were years ago. The number of divorce decrees in 1920 was 170,000. The postwar low point in the total number of divorces was reached in 1958 (368,000), while in 1967 the figure was 523,000, or an increase of 42.1 percent. The estimates for 1968 and 1969 were 582,000, and 660,000, respectively. [9]

Divorce in California

It is sometimes alleged that the state of California, for a host of reasons, including its concentration of entertainment industry personnel, has a divorce rate far beyond that of the rest of the nation. [10] Moreover, the implication seems to be that California is a kind of bellwether when it comes to marriage and divorce—that what is going on there now signals what will soon happen to most other states. However, California's pattern of rises and declines in divorce aproximates quite closely the national pattern shown in Figure 1.1. [11] It is true, however, that California's crude divorce rate has for some years surpassed the national rate by about 1.0 per 1000, so that in the mid-sixties, California's crude rate was 3.3, compared with the nation's 2.5. [12] But this difference is hardly catastrophic and, given the weakness in the crude rate discussed earlier, may be artificial. When a comparison is made for the same period between the national *refined* divorce rate and a comparable estimated rate for California, there is very little difference between the state and the nation, though the state figure remains slightly higher. [13] In short, while California may have a divorce rate slightly beyond that of the nation as a whole, there is no evidence to support the claim that California poses a "special case" of marital disintegration toward which America as a whole is moving.

Desertion

A very important factor to keep in mind when considering the century-long increase in American divorces is that decades ago many unsatisfac-

8. Plateris, 1970, p. 1.
9. Plateris, December, 1970, p. 1.
10. As an example, *see* Downing, p. 121.
11. *Divorce in California: 1966,* pp. 7–8.
12. *Ibid.,* p. 8.
13. *Ibid.,* p. 9.

tory marriages were broken by desertion rather than divorce.[14] The great masses of people simply could not afford the legal costs of divorce and so took a simpler way out. Incidentally, since only the economically well-off could afford divorce, this led to the widely held generalization that marital dissatisfaction and disruption were more frequent among the more economically advantaged, when very likely it was not. But since an accurate count of desertions among the less well-off was virtually impossible to obtain, the notion persisted. In the last few decades, with a general rise in income for most Americans, it has become possible for an increasing number of persons at most income levels to afford divorce. Therefore it is likely that the incidence of *actual unsatisfactory marriages* has not increased as greatly as Figure 1.1 might suggest. Where such marriages, especially among the less advantaged, were once ended informally by desertion, they may now be ended formally by legal decree.

CURRENT MARRIAGE TO CURRENT DIVORCE RATIO

Both the crude and the refined rates are far superior to the marriage-divorce ratio that is so often quoted and which seems to be the prime basis for the allegation that American marriage is coming apart. The marriage-divorce ratio should be labeled, "how *not* to measure the incidence of divorce." On the surface it seems appealingly simple. Let us say that in any metropolitan area last month there were 1,000 marriage licenses issued. During that same month there were 250 divorce decrees issued. If we simply compare the two numbers we conclude that for every four marriages there is one divorce, and that at least 25 percent of all marriages will eventually end in divorce. For in the United States as a whole, as in our hypothetical metropolitan area, it is true that for every 1,000 marriages consummated in any given year, there are approximately 250 divorce decrees.

However, as Plateris points out, there are two major reasons why this kind of comparison is a spurious one and ought to be discarded.[15] The first is based on the fact that almost all divorces in any given year are allowed to persons who were married in *preceding* years—from one to twenty-five years previous in most cases. Gross errors are introduced when the divorces of people who were married, say, anywhere from 1945 to 1970, are compared with those marriages consummated in 1971. This is chiefly because the composition (age distribution, and so on) of the population married during any one year is substantially different from the composition of the population married over a wide range of earlier years.[16]

14. Winch, 1971.
15. Plateris, 1967, pp. 2–3. *See also* Goode, 1963, pp. 81–82.
16. Plateris, 1967.

Besides being an inaccurate and therefore invalid comparison, Plateris dryly points out that if this kind of ratio is used as the basis for prediction, it can be reduced to an absurdity.[17] For if, using this technique, we predict, as is so often done, that one out of four marriages will end in divorce, what do we predict about the three remaining? The fact is that in any given year, compared to every 1,000 new marriages, there are also approximately 500 marriages from earlier years that are dissolved by death, as well as 250 earlier marriages dissolved by divorce. May we then predict that one out of every four marriages will end in divorce, and that two out of every four will end in death? But since the remaining one in four cannot go on forever, what kind of prediction can we make about its termination? Since it must end at some point in time, such a technique of measuring divorce rates is clearly suspect and ought to be set aside. For the person, however, who had believed allegations that 25 percent (or more) of all marriages "end in divorce every year," it could be a shock to discard the unreliable current marriage-divorce ratio.

FOLLOWING MARRIAGE COHORTS OVER TIME

The most reliable and valid way to determine how many marriages eventually end in divorce would be to follow a national sample of marriages consummated in a given year until either divorce or death overtake them. No investigator has yet carried out an ambitious and expensive study of this sort. It would involve a "tracking" process in which each man and woman in the sample would be followed (no matter where they moved) from the time he obtained his marriage license through any and all separations, desertions, death of spouse, divorces, and remarriages until his own death. (This technique says nothing, of course, about persons who choose to live together regardless of legal formalities. That topic will be discussed in subsequent chapters.)

Nonetheless, in spite of the absence of that type of information we can, by looking retrospectively at data which has been collected for past marriages, get some idea of the likelihood of marital dissolution over the duration of marriages *up to this point in time*. In 1960:

> For ever-married persons 65 years of age and over (few of whom would marry again), 79 percent of the men and 84 percent of the women had been married only once. . . . For persons 55 to 64 years old, 81 percent of the men and 82 percent of the women had been married only once.[18]

In short, approximately four out of five marriages remain intact through middle-age and beyond. This means that before age sixty-five,

17. *Ibid.*
18. Carter and Glick, 1970, p. 83.

one out of five marriages is dissolved by *either* death *or* divorce, but not solely by the latter. Thus the likelihood of having a dissolved marriage over the length of the life cycle to age sixty-five seems to be about one in five. *But dissolution among that remaining 20 percent may be due to death as well as to divorce.* How much of that remaining proportion is due to divorce and how much to death? Present procedures for collection and reporting these kinds of data make it difficult to answer that question precisely. However, a 1967 study of a national sample of Americans found that of all ever-married persons under seventy years of age, 15 percent of the men and 17 percent of the women had been divorced.[19] Thus, of that approximately 20 percent of persons with a not-intact first marriage, the majority apparently lost their spouses by divorce rather than death.

At the same time, even those figures can be deceptive if we fail to take into account the variable of race. Only 14 percent of ever-married white men under seventy experienced divorce as compared to 28 percent of black men. The figures for white and black women are 15 and 32 percent, respectively.[20] Furthermore, as we shall see later in the chapter, these latter figures can also be misleading unless we take account of both age at marriage and socioeconomic factors. The global question "How many American marriages end in divorce," could produce a spurious answer if we stopped there. One must go on and specify how many marriages among black and how many among white Americans end in divorce. How many young versus mature marriages end in divorce? How many working-class versus middle-class marriages end in divorce?

TRENDS IN MARITAL DISSOLUTION THROUGH DEATH

In trying to answer the question as to whether or not American marriage is disintegrating, we must also look briefly at the substantial reductions in American death rates during the last hundred years. Throughout most of the nineteenth century, it was not uncommon for a male to lose several wives, mostly through fatal infections acquired in the course of frequent childbearing. Moreover, both men and women had much shorter life expectancies than at present. Consequently marriages generally tended to be of much shorter duration than they are today. Dissatisfactions in marriage that today might lead to divorce had perhaps less chance then to build up and bring about divorce, since death might intervene beforehand. Hence, some unsatisfactory kinds of marriages which are today being dissolved by divorce might have been dissolved "naturally" through death.

In 1963, for instance, for every 1,000 existing marriages some 19.1

19. Glick and Norton, 1971, p. 309.
20. *Ibid.*

ended by death, while only 9.6 ended by divorce, a total of 28.7 marital dissolutions.[21] In any given year, therefore, marital dissolution due to death is about twice as great as dissolution due to divorce. In 1860, while the "refined" divorce rate was 1.2, the number of marriages dissolved by death was 28.4 per 1,000 existing marriages. Hence, the 1860 total of 29.6 marriages being dissolved yearly due to both factors combined was actually greater than the 1963 total of 28.7. In fact, because of decreasing death rates, the long-range trend between 1860 and 1963 shows a steady decrease in number of actual yearly total marital dissolutions due to *both factors combined*. This point is important in assessing whether marital patterns as we know them are being repudiated by American society. *It seems safe to conclude that more Americans are spending more years in the marital situation than ever before in our history.* If there were any widespread "breakdown" of conjugal patterns, then we might expect a reversal of the foregoing generalization. But, due chiefly to decreasing death rates, Carter and Glick conclude:

> Among men, nearly 68 percent of the entire life in 1964, as compared with only 59 percent in 1940, was spent as a married man with wife present. Among women, the corresponding figures were about 62 percent in 1964 and 50 percent in 1940.[22]

ANNUAL PROBABILITY DIVORCE RATE

The most recently developed measure of marital dissolution and perhaps the most valid is the "annual probability divorce rate." It tells us what are the chances of a person's (man or woman, black or white) becoming divorced during any particular year of his *first* marriage.[23]

Comparison of the 1950s with the 1960s shows very little change between them in the annual probability of divorce, whether we look at men or women, whites or blacks. In the sixties, the overall chances that an American male would become divorced anytime during the first through the twenty-sixth year of his *first* marriage were 7 for every 1,000 such married men. For every 1,000 once-married men, in short, 7 actually became divorced. Among white men, however, only 6 out of 1,000 actually experienced divorce. For black men the chances were almost double—11 of every 1,000 black husbands obtained a divorce. In the fifties the chances that a white man would be divorced were 7 out of 1,000; for a black man they were 13 out of 1,000. Among all women in both decades the chances were 7 out of 1,000; the same figure applied to white women in both decades; and for black women the chances were 13 out of 1,000 in the

---

21. Winch, 1971
22. 1970, p. 64. We shall discuss remarriages in chapter three.
23. *Current Population Reports*, P–23, No. 32.

fifties and 10 out of 1,000 in the sixties. It must be remembered also that, at any one point in time, the proportion of blacks who are married and yet *separated* from their spouses is much greater than it is for whites. In March, 1968, for instance, the percentage of ever-married white women who were separated from their husbands was 1.8 percent; for black women the figure was 11.9 percent.[24] The disparity in separation rates is probably owing to the high legal costs of divorce, which are often beyond the means of many lower-class blacks.

In sum, when comparing the chances for divorce anytime throughout the first twenty-six years of marriage, the annual percentage probability of divorce *in the first marriage* ranges from less than 1 percent to about 2 percent for whites and up to 3 percent for blacks. These percentages correspond closely to those discussed above in connection with the "refined" divorce rate. Hence if one had to describe the likelihood of divorce in the United States in general terms, these are the kinds of figures he might cite instead of the extravagant (and unreliable) numbers based on the current marriage to current divorce ratio.

No matter which of the reliable measures one might choose, it seems clear that there is no such thing as a "runaway divorce" rate in the United States. The continuing pattern, long established since 1860, seems to be one of a gradual but steady increase in divorce rates—with brief intermittent periods of decline or rise.

CROSS-NATIONAL COMPARISONS IN DIVORCE RATES

We shall return to the U.S. data, but first we need to examine divorce rates in other developed societies. We do this for two main reasons: one, the cross-national data will put the American situation in perspective and will help to reinforce the idea that no widespread marital disintegration exists either in the United States or in other developed countries. Second, the data will help to prepare the way for the explanations suggested in chapters two, three, and four to account for gradual, worldwide increases in divorce rates. For example, the crude divorce rate for the Soviet Union in 1960 was 1.3; in 1967, it was 2.74.[25] For Sweden in 1930 the rate was 0.36; in 1967 it was 1.36. In Austria, during the same period, the figure rose from 0.10 to 1.21; in Hungary, from 0.64 to 2.06; in Denmark, from 0.65 to 1.43; in Czechoslovakia, from 0.40 to 1.39; and so on for most other developed nations.

We find that when we compare nations, the U.S. had until 1965 the

24. *Current Population Reports,* P–20, No. 187.
25. Plateris, 1967, 1969.

highest divorce rate of any in the world, though during the fifties the rate for the United Arab Republic (Egypt) was higher, owing to the particular character of Arab divorce laws at that time.[26]

By 1966, the United States had lost the distinction of being first in this realm and was surpassed by the Soviet Union. In 1967, its crude divorce rate was 2.74, while the U.S. figure was 2.64. The question naturally arises if there are any forces specific to Russia which might account for their levels of divorce—forces besides those found in other developing societies. According to Geiger, the answer is "yes." [27]

Both for ideological and pragmatic reasons (Marxism–Leninism and rapid industrialization), it has been the *official policy* of the Soviet regime since the Revolution to induce genuine equality in male and female sex roles in both family and occupational structures. Other countries, such as Sweden, have officially, but gently and gradually, encouraged sex-role equality, but no other government (except perhaps Communist China's) has enforced it with such vigor as has Russia's:[28]

> . . . pressures for change in male and female sex roles [were imposed] so rapidly that there has not been enough time to assimilate them; consequently, conflicts have appeared in more raw and insoluble form. When the spouses occupy positions in which the wife has lost her allegiance to the peasant [or traditional] pattern and the husband is unwilling to grant an equal-rights relationship, frequent and explosive conflicts arise.[29]

We shall take up the Soviet situation again more fully in chapter five. In passing, we simply note that while the Soviet government officially encourages sex-role equality, it officially discourages marital dissolution through extraordinarily strict divorce laws and exorbitantly high legal fees for divorce. Several observers comment that were it not for these kinds of extremely formidable legal and financial obstacles, ". . . the crude divorce rate of the USSR might well have been twice or three times as high. . . ." [30] In the rural areas, it is apparently quite common for persons who wish to divorce and marry someone else simply to stop living with the undesirable partner and start living with the more desirable one—all without the complication of legal formalities.[31]

When he tried to put the rates for a large number of countries in perspective, Plateris developed what he calls a "ratio of increase" in

26. Goode, 1963, pp. 155, 157.
27. Geiger, 1968, pp. 240ff.
28. Dahlström, pp. 170ff.
29. Geiger, p. 248.
30. *Ibid.*, p. 258.
31. *Ibid.*

divorce between 1930 and 1963. For example, the ratio of increase for the U.S. was 1.4. The only countries having a smaller or equal "ratio of increase" were France, Switzerland, West Germany, and the Netherlands, where their ratio increases were 1.3 or 1.4. Most other nations had substantially larger increases in this ratio—the largest being 25.0 for Venezuela, 11.4 for Austria, 7.4 for England and Wales, 5.1 in both Canada and Rumania, and 5.0 for Mexico.[32]

It would appear that while the U.S. continues its century-old gradual upswing in crude divorce rates, other countries that started this trend much later are "catching up" through a "ratio of growth" in an incidence of divorce much greater than our own.

A major implication of this discussion, however, is that anyone who might allege the breakdown of American marriage because our divorce rates are among the world's highest must also, to be honest, first point out our comparatively lower ratio of increase in divorces. Second, he must take note of the fact that at least one major industrialized nation has recently actually exceeded us in terms of the crude divorce rate and that other nations could do the same. It seems clear that there are cross-national forces that account for worldwide increases in divorce rates that are in no way unique to the United States.

VARIATIONS IN DISSOLUTION RATES

In trying to answer the central question of this chapter—to what extent do current divorce rates signal disintegration of dominant conjugal patterns—it is essential to recall that every married couple is not equally exposed to the same chances of experiencing dissolution.

THE FACTOR OF YOUTH

Refined Divorce Rate by Age at Divorce Decree

In Figure 1.1 we see that in 1965 for every 1,000 married women there were 10.6 divorces. (For men the rate was 10.8.) However that same year among every 1,000 married men in the U.S. under age 20, there were 27.1 divorces, or almost triple the national rate.[33] Among every 1,000 married men ages 20 to 24, there were 29 divorces, and 22 divorces among married men 25 to 29.[34] For every 1,000 married women under 20, there were 31 divorces—again almost triple the overall rate. The rate drops to 26 divorces among women 20 to 24, and to 18 for women 25 to 29.[35]

32. Plateris, 1967, p. 7.
33. Plateris, 1969, p. 26.
34. *Ibid.*
35. *Ibid.*

Clearly, therefore, merely saying that the refined divorce rate is 10 or 11 fails to represent the actual situation fully enough. It is men and women under 25 who have the highest divorce rates of any age group in the population. At the same time, we must remember that even 30 divorces, or 3 percent per thousand married is not generally construed as a large percentage. Even among the young the overwhelming majority each year remain married.

Age at Marriage

Even more significant than age at divorce is how old the divorced were when they first got married. In 1965, the median age at marriage for all American males was 22.8 years; for females it was 20.6 years.[36] We may then ask, how likely is it that persons who marry below the national median will become divorced? For females the chances are extremely high —almost 1 in 2—because in 1965, 48 percent of all wives involved in divorce had been married below age 20.[37] While for men that relationship is more ambiguous, it is clear that when a woman marries before age 20 (still in her teens) or below the average age at which most women marry, she is running an extraordinarily high risk of separation and eventual divorce.

In 1967, it was found that of all ever-married white women under seventy who had been married 20 years or more, 25 percent of those who had been divorced had been married for the first time between ages 14 to 19; only 13 percent had been first married between ages 20 to 24; and 12 percent were first married at ages 25 and over. For black women, the figures are 47, 31, and 32 percent, respectively.[38] For white men of that age and marriage length, 25 percent of those divorced were first married between ages 14 to 21; 13 percent were first married between ages 22 to 27; 10 percent at ages 28 and over. For black men, the figures are 46, 31, and 25 percent, respectively. Put another way, the annual chances of being divorced are 17 out of 1,000 among white men during years 5 to 9 of their first marriage if they were first married between ages 14 to 19. The chances drop by more than half to 8 out of 1,000 if they were married between ages 20 to 29.[39]

Clearly, to be married at a young age is to be at extraordinarily high risk in terms of marital dissolution. But why the association? Do the young love less than those who are older? If anything, we would expect them to be greatly caught up in the novelties and passions of sexual

36. *Current Population Reports,* P–20, No. 212, p. 1.
37. Plateris, 1969, p. 29.
38. Glick and Norton, p. 309.
39. *Ibid.*

experimentation and "young love." However it is not the variable of youth alone that has such a negative impact on marital stability: the effects of young marriage cannot be understood apart from the effects of class differences.

THE FACTOR OF SOCIAL DIFFERENTIATION

It is a common error to assume that divorce and separation occur most often among those who are economically well off. We have already discussed one historical reason for the emergence of this misconception, and another is the great publicity given to divorces of Hollywood stars whose incomes are usually extremely high. But out of 207,000,000 Americans, the total number of such persons is *statistically* insignificant. If we want to get the picture for the society as a whole, then we must look at the incidence of divorce at all class levels. This, however, does not imply that marital dissolution within the entertainment industry is not *theoretically* significant, as we shall see in chapter five.

Educational Level and Stability

During the first four years of marriage (the period when the greatest proportion of divorces occur) the white men most likely to experience divorce are those with fewer than eight years of education. Their average annual chances are 17 out of 1,000. If they have 8 to 11 years of education, their annual chances of divorce drop to 16; if 12 years of education, the chances drop to 12 in 1,000; but if they have 13 to 15 years of education, their chances rise to 15 in 1,000. By far the lowest chances for divorce are among men with 16 or more years of education: 6 chances out of 1,000.[40] A similar pattern appears for black men.[41] Thus, while we might say that in general the more education a man gets, the better are his chances for marital stability, there is an exception among high school graduates who attend but do not complete college. Their chances for dissolution are greater than high school graduates who do not attend college. Why this should be is not totally clear, but below we shall discuss a possible reason. Among women, however, white and black, the pattern is more consistent.[42] The annual chances for divorce among white women high school graduates during the third to fifth year of marriage are 13 out of 1,000; with 13 to 15 years of education, the chances are 8 out of 1,000; for 16 years or more, the chances are 2 out of 1,000. For black women, the chances are 20, 3, and 1, respectively. We may therefore

---

40. Glick and Norton, pp. 315ff.
41. *Current Population Reports*, P–20, No. 223.
42. *Ibid.*

conclude that in general (except for male college dropouts who yet have less chance for divorce than those without a high school diploma), education and marital stability are positively related: the more education a person has, the more likely he or she is to remain married to his or her first spouse.

Husband's Occupational Status and Stability

In 1960 91 percent of once-married men were employed, but only 69 and 70 percent of separated and divorced men, respectively, were employed. Of men with stable marriages, 33 percent hold white-collar jobs, but only 13 percent of the separated and 19 percent of the divorced hold these higher level positions. Moreover there is evidence to show that professionals are more likely to be living with their first wives, less likely to experience separation or divorce than are lower-level white collar workers.[43] Similarly, among the blue-collar ranks, craftsmen, skilled workers, and foremen are more likely to have stable marriages than are unskilled or semiskilled workers.[44] We may conclude that in addition to education, the greater the occupational status of the husband, the more likely he is to experience a stable marriage.

Husband's Income and Stability

Also in 1960 only 48 percent of men living with their first wives had annual incomes of less than $5,000, whereas 81 percent of separated men and 71 percent of divorced men had that low level of income. At the other extreme, 24 percent of once-married men had an income of $7,000 or more, while only 7 percent of separated men and 11 percent of divorced men had an income that high. Income, in fact, appears to be a more powerful predictor of marital stability than either education or husband's job status, particularly early in marriage. For example, the average annual chances of a white man to be divorced were 29 out of 1,000 during the fifth to ninth year of his first marriage if he earned less than $3,000 in 1966. If his income was $3,000 to $4,999, the chances dropped dramatically to 12; the chances were 11 out of 1,000 if he earned $5,000 to $7,999; and were only 6 out of 1,000 if his income was over $8,000.[45] A similar association is found for black husbands.[46] Like education and occupation, therefore, the higher the husband's income, the greater the likelihood of marital stability and the fewer the chances for separation and divorce.

43. Carter and Glick, p. 209.
44. *Ibid.*
45. Glick and Norton, p. 315.
46. *Current Population Reports*, P–20, No. 223.

Socioeconomic Position and Marital Stability

If we assume that education, job status, and income are indicators of class position, then it is clear that social class and separation-divorce are inversely related. This is true not just in the United States, but in most other developed lands such as Sweden, Belgium, France, England, Japan, Australia, New Zealand, and so forth.[47] Social differentiation remains in the Soviet Union, and there too the less advantaged classes experience less marital stability than those more economically advantaged.[48] It would appear that most countries, *once they reach the mature stages of modernization* and thus become similar to the United States in social structure, tend to develop a similar positive relationship between economic position and marital stability.

The marriage and family system of a society is inextricably related to that society's economic system; and we cannot understand the past, present, or future structures of the family until we make explicit its linkages to the larger society through the economic system. For example, in looking at the present state of marriage to determine whether or not it is breaking down, the overrepresentation of the divorced among the less advantaged, and their underrepresentation among those better off, suggests several ideas. First, there are forces *outside* of marriage that have much to do with whether marriages remain intact or not. Hence, rather than look for "weaknesses" within family structure, we ought to concentrate on those external forces that substantially influence it. We should no longer be preoccupied with a nonexistent notion—widespread marital disintegration—but instead with *how* and *why* factors such as education, occupation, and income influence marital stability.

For instance, how does social position explain why age is related to marital instability? Bartz and Nye found that "the lower the social class, the more likely early marriage will occur." [49] Persons from less advantaged backgrounds tend to marry younger than persons from more advantaged backgrounds. Why this should be is not completely clear, but Bartz and Nye suggest that it has to do with the array of options and rewards open to persons from varied strata.[50] Adolescents from more advantaged homes have the option, for example, of college and the immediate and long-range rewards that higher education promises. Thus, there is more motivation to pursue these kinds of rewards and put off marriage in lieu of them. Conversely, those lacking this option and its rewards may be much

---

47. Goode, 1966, in Bendix and Lipset.
48. Geiger, pp. 250–51.
49. Bartz and Nye, p. 266.
50. Bartz and Nye, pp. 258ff.

more likely to seek the option and the immediate rewards of a youthful marriage.

And, "the earlier the marriage, the more likely the lower social class placement of the couple." [51] That is, younger couples who begin marriage with less economic advantage subsequently find it more difficult to take advantage of educational and occupational opportunities that might enable them as persons and as a couple to become socially mobile—i.e., to exceed the occupational levels of their parents. Younger age at marriage is associated with dropping out of high school or not taking training beyond high school. The relative lack of education means fewer economic resources for the marriage, so that within the first ten years many of these marriages are dissolved.[52]

Second is the relationship of premarital pregnancy to age at marriage and to economic disadvantage in marriage. There are several studies indicating that regardless of the social class of their parents persons who became involved with premarital pregnancy tend to marry earlier than those who do not, and they also tend to attain less education. Schor notes, from national data, that at least two factors negative to marital stability arise from that kind of situation.[53] (1) Young persons with necessarily limited income-producing potential find that it is difficult to stretch minimal dollars to provide for medical and other costs of the pregnant mother, and subsequently, to afford all the needs for an "extra" person. (2) Couples who marry young and have their first child soon after marriage are very likely to have more total children over the family cycle than are other American families. Thus they begin with severe income deficiencies, and these deficiencies are compounded yearly as a result of low-income production and a comparatively large number of children to feed, clothe, house, and otherwise provide for.

Some rather convincing evidence for the association between premarital conception, age at marriage, and disadvantaged economic position has been gathered by the U.S. Public Health Service for the years 1964–66. First, they make the assumption that a birth anytime within the first eight months of marriage was conceived prior to legal union. On that basis, during those calendar years, in America, 42.4 percent of all legitimate births to married women 15 to 19 years old were premaritally conceived; but the figure drops dramatically to 14.5 percent for women aged 20 to 24; to 3.7 percent for women aged 25 to 29; and to 1.7 percent for ages 30 to 34.[54]

51. Bartz and Nye, p. 266.
52. The details of the *process* of dissolution or stability are described in chapter four.
53. Schor, 1968. *See also* Baumann, 1967; Coombs, 1970.
54. *Monthly Vital Statistics Report,* March, 1970.

Next, among married women whose family incomes were under $3,000, 38 percent of first births were conceived prior to marriage. When the income was $3,000 to 4,999, the premarital conception figure was 23 percent; for $5,000 to 6,999 incomes the figure was 18 percent; it was 12 percent for incomes of $7,000 to 9,999; and 8 percent for incomes $10,000 and over.[55] Finally, among all married women with four years or more of college, only 7.5 percent of their first births were premaritally conceived. With one to three years of college, the figure was 18.1 percent; four years of high school, 20.7 percent; one to three years of high school, 31.6 percent; elementary school, 21.2 percent.[56]

Youth, therefore, is not by itself inimical to marriage. There are many nonmodern cultures where it is a common occurrence. But in a modern society to marry young, owing to pregnancy or for any reason, is to reduce the chances for gaining further education, which subsequently reduces the level of social and economic resources available to the marriage during its first ten years—precisely those years when most separations and divorces occur.[57] And as we have seen, the fewer economic resources a marriage possesses, the more difficult it is to maintain that marriage.

By definition, there can be no marriage without some level of economic interdependence:

> Sexual unions without economic cooperation are common, and there are relationships between men and women involving a division of labor without sexual gratification . . . but marriage exists only when the economic and the sexual are united into one relationship, and this combination occurs only in marriage.[58]

This is the definition of marriage that we shall follow throughout this book. It is exceedingly parsimonious and flexible in that the form or structure of the economic and sexual (or expressive) relations could theoretically take any conceivable shape whatsoever, including polygynous or group marriage. It is also broad enough to subsume communal arrangements, as well as homosexual or lesbian relationships. All that is required is that the persons (whatever their number) in the marriage maintain both types of interdependencies.

Lower-class blacks in America represent a segment of the population which has been bypassed by the economic advances of recent decades. And it is within that stratum of society that the highest levels of marital dissolution to be found anywhere in our society are located. In short,

55. *Ibid.*
56. *Ibid.*
57. *See* Cutright, 1971, who argues that income is more *directly* critical to marital stability than either education or occupation, which influence income.
58. Murdock, p. 8.

access to the economic system and its resources in large measure determine chances for marital stability. Does it then follow that if more males have access to greater levels of education and to higher job status and income that the incidence of marital instability would decline? Parke and Glick predict that this is indeed the case.[59] They predict that as the American economy expands and more men have opportunities for better education and jobs, separation and divorce rates should level off and perhaps decline.

THE FACTOR OF RACE

Socioeconomic position will influence black rates of marital stability more adversely than white rates, for the precise reason that blacks have fewer economic resources than whites. It is important that this be understood because of the confusion emerging from stereotypes that many whites have about black families in America. American blacks live in families whose behaviors are differentiated chiefly by social class level as is true of whites.[60] Available evidence also indicates that the vast majority of blacks (even the poorest) know about and prefer the conjugal form of marriage.[61] Where they are not able to carry out this pattern, it is because of the economic discrimination they have suffered at the hands of white society. In 1968, 67 percent of metropolitan black households in the United States had *both* a husband and wife present, and less than 30 percent of black families were headed by a female, though this figure is greater than it was in 1960.[62] We have already looked at data showing that the chances for a black marriage to end in divorce are greater than those for a white marriage. At every income level black men are less likely than whites to be living with their first wives. For example, in 1960 among husbands between ages 25 to 34 with incomes up to $1,999, 70 percent of whites, compared with 62 percent of blacks, were still living with their first wives.[63] When the income is $1,000 to $2,999, the percentages are 80 to 71, respectively. When income is $3,000 to 4,999, the percentages are 87 and 78; at $5,000 to 6,999, they are 90 and 82; at $7,000 to $9,999, they are 91 and 83; at $10,000 or more, they are 92 and 82, respectively. Similar results emerge when comparisons are made by occupation or education.[64] However, as these figures show, as black income rises, marital stability increases as it does for whites and as it does in other developed countries. It is clear for black marriages, as for mar-

59. Parke and Glick, 1967.
60. Scanzoni, 1971.
61. Rainwater, 1966.
62. *Current Population Reports,* P–23, No. 27.
63. Cutright, 1971, p. 295.
64. Udry, 1966.

riages generally in industrial society, that the more socioeconomic resources they possess the more likely they are to remain stable.

Moreover, the differences in frequency of stability between blacks and whites at the same income levels are not due to any "weakness" (cultural or otherwise) in black family structure, but to what has been termed *relative deprivation*. That is, despite the publicity given to the "frantic search" to hire black college graduates, on the national level blacks with education equal to whites experience discrimination that leads consistently to lower job status.[65] And even if blacks are allowed to obtain a job with equal status to whites, blacks consistently earn less money, according to national census data.[66] In other words, many black men achieve comparatively "good" educational and job positions, but are denied the rewards and benefits that are given to whites with similar achievements.

For example, a black man and a white man may each be earning $8,000 annually. But the white man may simply have finished high school and be working at a blue-collar job commensurate with his level of education. It is quite possible that the black man may have several years of college, but owing to job discrimination, he is unable to obtain a job and income commensurate with his educational attainments. Perhaps all he can find is a blue-collar job, far below, in both status and income, the kinds of jobs that most similarly educated white men obtain. This relative deprivation compared to whites of equal education, multiplied many times over, contributes in large measure to the greater frequency of black marital instability even above the lower class.

The concept of relative deprivation, incidentally, may be at the core of the pattern observed above, in which high school graduates (blacks and whites) who do not attempt college have less chance for marital instability than those who make the attempt but drop out. Husbands (and their wives) in the latter category may have had aspirations for a life-style that is commensurate with that usually obtained by persons who graduate from college. Thus they compare themselves with college graduates rather than with high school graduates. But since their income leads to a life-style more like that of high school graduates, they may feel "relatively deprived." That is, they had hoped for the life-style of the college graduate but were not able to obtain it, and thus by comparison feel very dissatisfied. The high school graduate (and his wife), on the other hand, may feel more satisfied than his erstwhile peers with the attainment of a lower level of aspirations, and thus feel less relatively deprived. Hence, the feelings of relative deprivation experienced by husbands and wives of

65. Scanzoni, 1971, chapter 5.
66. *Ibid.*

some "drop-out" marriages may in turn negatively influence their expressive behaviors, and thus increase the chances for dissolution compared to less aspiring high school graduates.

The element of relative deprivation, along with the extreme poverty experienced by at least one-quarter to one-third of black society, helps to account for the finding that 29 percent of black households are headed by a female, as compared to 8 percent of white households. As seen earlier in the chapter, since blacks often cannot afford legal means to terminate marriage, separation is much more common among them than among whites.

We saw earlier that the relatively disadvantaged tend to marry earlier than those who are better off. It follows that blacks, who are considerably more disadvantaged than whites, will tend to marry earlier. In 1969, of all married white males over age 18, 11.7 percent were married prior to age 20, but 14.1 percent of all black married males were married prior to that age.[67] Twenty percent of all black married females had married before age 18, while only 14.4 percent of white married females had wed prior to age 18. Thus to be black, economically disadvantaged, and young—*all three factors coalesce in one relatively small segment (12 percent) of the population* to account for their disproportionately higher rates of marital instability.

Moreover, we also saw that young age at marriage is often complicated by premarital conceptions which have a negative effect on the educational and economic resources that the couple is able to attain. Using the same criterion of premarital conception as above, during the period 1964–66, 20 percent of all white legitimate births were conceived prior to marriage, whereas 42 percent of all black legitimate births were so conceived.[68] Thus whatever difficulties are faced by any American marriage as a result of being in these kinds of "have-to" situations, they are exacerbated for the black population.

THE FACTOR OF HYPOCRISY: STABILITY WITHOUT SATISFACTION

It is legitimate to ask whether persons from the middle-classes may be more disingenuous than those from the working and lower classes regarding husband-wife relationships. That is, do higher-status persons stay together in spite of unsatisfactory interpersonal or expressive relationships, because of certain social and job pressures or fear of scandal, and thus are hypocritical about their marriages?[69] Perhaps, but probably not, because of another set of findings that emerges consistently in the research

67. *Current Population Reports*, P–20, No. 198, p. 2.
68. *Monthly Vital Statistics Report*, March 25, 1970.
69. *See* Cutright, 1971, on the relation of "constraint" to marital stability.

literature: persons (white or black) with higher socioeconomic status are more apt than persons with lesser status to report satisfaction with the expressive components of marriage.

The evidence indicates that higher status is correlated with a more positive evaluation of those expressive elements (love, physical affection, companionship, empathy) that are presumably the core of modern marriage.[70] The assumption is, therefore, that less satisfaction with expressive behavior is associated with a greater willingness to dissolve the marriage. Being more satisfied is related to a stronger tendency to maintain the marriage.

But it is also legitimate to inquire whether higher status people prevaricate to interviewers about their evaluations of husband-wife expressiveness. Are they actually very dissatisfied, but lie nonetheless in order to maintain a "socially desirable front"? No doubt there is a tendency for persons at any status level to tend to give the "socially desirable" response to any sensitive question that an interviewer might put to him. On the other hand, there are three grounds for accepting the notion that social class and marital satisfaction are actually positively related.

The first pertains to the absence of stigma attached to marital dissolution in modern society. The notion that higher status persons are hypocritical about their marital situation rests in part on the traditional belief that divorced persons have somehow lapsed morally, that to be divorced is to be suspect, and therefore, among other things, not worthy of added responsibilities in one's business or profession. Most sociologists agree, however, that this particular orientation has virtually disappeared from contemporary society.[71]

Keep in mind, nonetheless, the statement that there is "no contemporary society, primitive or industrialized, in which divorce is actually valued." [72] While dissolution is not considered a "positive good" even by the lowest strata in American society, it is widely utilized as a means of "tension release." [73] Where once in Western society the prevailing norm was to make the best of a marriage, no matter how difficult, now American couples have become increasingly disinclined to suffer marriages that are unhappy. There is no reason to think that more advantaged persons have adopted this shift from a permanent to a pragmatic view of marriage any less strongly than the less advantaged. With the passing of the stigma, persons at all class levels are just as likely to resort to dissolution if the marital situation is not rewarding or too costly. "Middle-class hypocrisy,"

---

70. Hicks and Platt; Blood and Wolfe; Scanzoni, 1970 and 1971.
71. Goode, 1963, p. 81; Bernard, 1970, in Bohannan, p. 3; Farber, 1964.
72. Goode, 1966, p. 380, in Bendix and Lipset; Bernard, 1970, in Bohannan, pp. 3ff.
73. Rainwater, 1966.

therefore, does not seem to account for the patterns of satisfaction and stability that emerge consistently.

Second, on methodological grounds, some forty years of survey research in America and elsewhere give no indication whatsoever that *any* certain grouping in the population consistently falsifies information on any particular topic. Quite the contrary, all available evidence points toward remarkable candor on such "private and intimate" matters as politics, religion, sex, contraception, money, family interaction, and so on. The trained, anonymous interviewer with a well-constructed interview schedule seems quite capable of obtaining reasonably valid information from informants who are rarely hostile.

Finally, the most crucial reason of all for accepting the relative validity of the relationships in question is theoretical. The numerous studies from the United States and other Western nations all suggest a coherent theoretical framework to explain family structure. Some of the key points in this framework are basic to much current sociological endeavor: from a structural viewpoint the impact of social differentiation on virtually all aspects of human behavior, complementary to this from the cultural standpoint, the great value our society places on achievement and success, with success being evidenced in terms of material acquisitiveness and display of consumption symbols. The notion of social differentiation implies that some segments of society enjoy more benefits than do other segments.

In our society, part of these differential benefits are material in nature. Correlated with these benefits is a vast array of phenomena including mental health, physical well-being, educational and job opportunities, protection from the draft or from combat, and so on. It would appear, in fact, that there is even a correlation between "marital problems" and health problems:

> The available data, with some exceptions, support the thesis that serious trouble with health tends to be associated with serious trouble in becoming married, in maintaining a viable marriage, or in becoming remarried. These troubles evidently tend to be compounded by unfavorable economic adjustment.[74]

Just about every meaningful aspect of life in modern society is linked with social differentiation.[75] Those who rank higher on the class ladder generally tend to experience more of the "correlated benefits" proffered by society than those who rank lower. There is no reason to suppose that

74. Carter and Glick, p. 409.
75. *See* "Status and Satisfaction" and "Toward a Redefinition of Well-Being" in Miller and Roby, 1970.

family structure would be exempt from this core characteristic of modern society. On the contrary, one would predict that the most "rewarding" (from the standpoint of those involved) kinds of family patterns would be found most often among those who otherwise possess the basic benefits and rewards of the society.

CONCLUSION

Our objective in this chapter has been to determine whether available evidence indicates that the family system in America and in Western society in general is in a process of disorganization, breakdown, or collapse. There have been gradual, long-term increases in divorce rates in the United States and elsewhere. However, when looking at valid ways to assess these rates, they would appear (1) to be comparatively low; and (2) to be largely accounted for by the young, the less well off, and the black, a trilogy of variables that are often found together.

From these perspectives, the allegation of widespread "marital breakdown" is, at this time, virtually impossible to justify. Nor has the alleged chain of factors between divorce and *permanent* personal trauma, or "societal decay," ever been clearly spelled out and demonstrated.

Nonetheless, to suggest that the notion of marital disintegration is invalid in no way implies that the conjugal family as we know it may not be becoming irrelevant or passé. Especially among the young, or the divorced, or the blacks, or "women's lib," or "gay" groups, new forms of the family may be emerging that will make the present forms relatively outmoded, or at least vie with them for acceptance and significance.

II. Marriage in the Process of Change

While in chapter one the major emphasis was on the absence of marital disintegration, we now make explicit what so far has merely been implicit: the presence of continuing, long-term changes in marital structure. To say that marriage is not disintegrating is *not* to say that it has been, or is static. Quite the contrary is true. To try to describe these changes we shall, in this chapter, first of all, place the information and conclusions from the prior chapter into some sort of historical perspective. Why has there been this century-long increase in divorce rates in the United States? Why do divorce rates rise in other countries as they too follow us along the path to modernization? In short, what is it about modernization that accounts for *changes upward* in rates of marital dissolution?

Second, we want to show how that kind of change is part of the larger question of marital conflict and change in general. Since about 1800 certain forces have been at work that have generated substantial *conflict* within marital structure. The major consequence has been *change* in this structure; and historical perspective will make this plain. We will try to trace continuous conflict and change from 1800 up to and through the present and to set the stage for a discussion of current conflicts and changes related to "women's liberation" and future family forms.

COERCION OF THE WOMAN

Both Marx and Engels had much to say about marriage and its intrinsic connection to the economic system. Engels believed that the condition of man prior to the development of civilization was "primitive and natural collectivism." [1] And, argues Engels, marriage as we know it came

1. Engels, 1968, pp. 45ff.

about through "the subjugation of one by the other, as the proclamation of an antagonism between the sexes. . . . The first class antagonism in history and the first class oppression [was] that of the female by the male sex." [2]

One is not compelled to agree with all that Engels said in order to accept his central thesis—i.e., that males, because of their superior strength, over a long period of history effectively engulfed women into a system of marriage in which males enjoyed all or most of the available resources, rights, and privileges. Females, on the other side, were enjoined by numerous and binding duties and obligations. Nevertheless, Engels did not reject monogamous marriage per se. What Engels was against, of course, was the wage system and private ownership of property (including women as property) which, he said, make women dependent on men. "If one removes the economic considerations that now force women to submit to . . . men, women will be placed on an equal footing with men." According to Engels, once that type of economic element in marriage is removed, and women are equal with men, the only moral foundation for marriage that remains is love.

Murdock observes that since in virtually every known society sex relations are permitted outside of marriage, that "sex is an important, but not an exclusive, factor in maintaining the marital relationship. . . . Since economic cooperation, like sexual association, is most readily and satisfactorily achieved by persons who habitually reside together, the two activities, each deriving from a basic biological need, are quite compatible." [3] What began to emerge in most parts of the world was a situation in which men began to specialize in economic-occupational activities, women in nurturant and supportive activities. While in antiquity this may or may not have been a voluntary arrangement, it was not long before major civilizations such as the Hebrew, Greek, and Roman, and many tribes, codified it into law.

Not that the codification was initially based on rational calculation. As John Stuart Mill put it:

> The adoption of this system of inequality never was the result of deliberation, or forethought, or any social ideas, or any notion whatever of what conduced to the benefit of humanity or the good order of society. It arose simply from the fact that from the very earliest twilight of human society, every woman . . . was found in a state of bondage to some man. Laws . . . always begin by recognizing the relations they find already existing between individuals. They convert what was a mere physical fact into a legal right. [4]

2. *Ibid.*
3. Murdock, 1949, p. 8.
4. Mill, 1869, pp. 431–32.

What was the practical and behavioral result of this subjugation?

> Even the period of great license of imperial Rome during its decline did not give women [equality]. . . . In Rome, women had great freedom with respect to sexual behavior and divorce, but no range of important tasks was defined as open to them. . . . *Women were not permitted to do important tasks outside the home.*[5] [Italics supplied.]

If we think of roles as consisting of expectations of rights and duties, then we may say that historically men saw to it that in their roles, both in and out of the home, they themselves possessed most of the rights or privileges. At the same time they made sure that women's roles were structured chiefly in terms of duties or obligations. Throughout these epochs of world history, therefore, the relationship between male and female was essentially a coercive one, much like the relationship between whites and blacks since the beginning of the era of African slavery and colonialism. But coercion by itself does not necessarily imply conflict, particularly if the subordinate group is content to remain passive vis-à-vis the dominant group.

THE EMERGENCE OF MALE-FEMALE CONFLICT GROUPS

Historians seem to agree that for the first time "women emerged in the early nineteenth century as a distinct interest group."[6] This means that about that time some women became conscious of their deprivation *qua group* and sought to challenge and end the subjugation under which they had been collectively placed by men. *The challenge to this coercion may be described as a conflict relationship.* We may define conflict as "a struggle over values, behaviors, power, and resources, in which each opponent seeks to achieve his goals usually at some expense to the other."[7] How "expensive" one wishes to make the conflict for his challenger can be categorized in several ways. One type of conflict may be described as "zero-sum." In this conflict *A* wants to destroy *B* completely, e.g., the Allies vs. the Nazis in World War II. Far more common is the "mixed-motive" type of conflict (or game) in which, while *A* wants to gain certain objectives, it is decidedly in *A*'s best interest to see that *B* makes gains too, and conversely for *B*. For if either *A* or *B* is totally "wiped out," then his opponent stands to lose considerable benefits too.

Around 1800, therefore, the struggle or conflict between the interest groups of males and females was initiated by the subordinate group, since

5. Goode, 1963, pp. 55–56.
6. O'Neill, 1969, p. 15.
7. A variation on Coser's definition from his p. 8, 1956.

it is rarely in the interests of the dominant group ever to disturb the status quo. The specific interests and objectives of the subordinate group, as enunciated then, were clear enough: to remove all legal and social barriers to total equality between the sexes. The interests and objectives of the males were equally plain: to preserve the inequalities which they defined as "proper" and which benefited them.

According to Mary Beard, the legal inequities against which the early feminists reacted so strongly were traceable in large measure to the interpretations given to English common law by Sir William Blackstone in the eighteenth century.[8] Apparently his interpretations had enormous influence not only in England but also in the development of the legal system of the infant American republic, as laws began to be written for and applied to women. It was he, for instance, who argued that a wife is not an entity distinct or separate from her husband: her legal existence was suspended during marriage. She could not own property, sign a contract, or vote. Her legal personhood was totally swallowed up or covered by the name and authority of her husband.

Arising from this extinguishment of the woman's autonomy was the issue of control over her person and body. Since the husband was totally responsible for his wife's actions and debts (she was *one* with him), he had the right to inflict "moderate" physical beatings upon her and to coerce her into sexual relations. She had no right to independent action. Therefore, when the early feminists began the conflict it was directed toward these general legal issues of autonomy and control and their many immediate implications in the writing and application of specific laws that influenced the total destinies of American and English women.

To describe males and females as interest groups in conflict does not imply that *every individual* male was, or is now, in conflict with *every individual* female. It is possible to look at the family through two levels of analysis. At one level, we may view the family as a major institution of society, and at another level, we may examine roles (and individuals occupying these roles) operating within the larger institution. It is at what Blau calls the macro or institution level that we conceive of conflicting male-female interest groups.[9] At the more micro level of role interaction, the essence of the husband-wife relationship is based on the attainment of interests, or reward-seeking, which may more accurately and fundamentally be described as a reciprocal, rather than a conflict, type association. Nevertheless, a permanent relationship based on reward-seeking inevitably, at times, erupts into conflict and may even sometimes become almost totally a conflict situation.

8. Beard, 1946, pp. 78ff. References to Blackstone on the text are taken from Beard.
9. *See* Blau, p. 24.

Before we can understand contemporary processes of husband-wife reciprocity and conflict, we need first to explore thoroughly the broader level of marriage as institution, characterized by the struggle between conflicting interest groups. This is so because the present structure of husband-wife role relations is the outcome of earlier struggles or conflicts. Similarly, the idea of conflict is central to an understanding of what present-day feminists mean when they argue that current family structure is not the end of the struggle and that it too needs to be changed to something different.

Why women gained a sense of "class consciousness" and began to conflict seriously with men over their social and legal status at the juncture of history subsequent to 1800 is a subject of dispute among historians.[10] Kraditor indicates that in the United States, at least, the "immediate cause" of the sense of class consciousness leading to the feminist movement "was the experience of a few women in the abolitionist movement . . . who found their religiously inspired work for the slave impeded by the prejudices against public activity for women. They and many others began to ponder the parallels between women's status and the Negro's status, and to notice that white men usually applied the principles of natural rights and the ideology of individualism only to themselves." [11] The fact that white males dominated the abolitionist movement and allowed females almost no power in its direction certainly helped to spawn the feminist movement in America.

However, converging with those specific experiences in abolitionism, were two more general and more fundamental factors that are now also at work today in most world societies. The first of these Goode describes as "the crucial crystalizing variable—i.e., the necessary but not sufficient cause of the betterment of the Western woman's position—was ideological: the gradual, logical, philosophical extension to women of originally Protestant notions about the rights and responsibilities of the *individual* undermined the traditional idea of 'woman's proper place'." [12]

Second, in addition to changes in values structural changes also took place that enabled women to effectively challenge male privileges. As Western societies industrialized and modernized, there developed

a free labor market, in which the individual was hired for his own skill, with little or decreasing regard for his family position. . . . The woman . . . no longer needed to depend on her family elders or males when she wanted to work. Consequently, she achieved an independent basis for her own existence, so that she could, in the larger society as well as in the

10. O'Neill, 1969, pp. 15ff.
11. Kraditor, pp. 13–14.
12. Goode, 1963, p. 56.

family, drive a better "role bargain." That is, she could achieve a better set of rights and obligations with respect to other statuses.[13]

What industrial society does is to strike down the ancient irreversibilities of *ascribed* roles—those gotten by birth; and open up the possibility of *achieved* roles—those gotten by individual attainments. Until modern times, women received their major gratifications or rewards by "pleasing" husband and children. There was, in that premodern setting, very little challenge or conflict to males and hence the status quo was maintained. Women acquiesced in their marital arrangements chiefly because there were few viable role alternatives available. On the other hand, husbands were quite content with the status quo and in no way impelled to challenge it, simply because they were enjoying traditional male rights, privileges, and prerogatives.

Modern society provides the kinds of conditions under which women are able to challenge (conflict with) male privileges. To some degree in marriage, and especially in other segments of the society, women began to seek rewards besides the well-being of spouse and offspring: they also began to seek rewards for themselves as individual persons. We cannot discuss the full range of conflicts waged by the early feminists to achieve legal equalities and especially suffrage. Accounts of those struggles are readily available.[14] Instead, our attention will be centered on *how* those conflicts, borne by ideas of surging individualism and personal freedom, plus an ever-expanding labor market, were related to conflicts and changes within marriage. In this regard, we must admit that our knowledge of nineteenth-century family patterns must rely on historical accounts of uncertain validity, since more rigorously compiled data was not available until sometime into the twentieth century. Gordon and Bernstein, for example, analyzed nineteenth-century marriage manuals and concluded that "the wife's role can be characterized as . . . an 'obedience-submissive-reverence' complex, and the husband's role complements this, i.e., he is a benign despot." [15]

Furstenberg has attempted to organize what appear to be some of the best historical materials available that describe the American family of the last century. His conclusions support the notion that married women during that period possessed few rights:

> The aspect of married life which drew the most attention [of visiting European scholars, including Tocqueville] was the great loss of freedom the woman suffered when she married. . . . Married women suffered unnecessary discrimination. . . . After consenting to marry [they] had little

13. *Ibid.*, pp. 56–57.
14. O'Neill, 1969.
15. Gordon and Bernstein, p. 665.

left to bargain with. . . . There were really no alternatives open to the women which would permit them to get out of the home. . . . [They had] demanding domestic obligations. . . . women occupy an inferior position in American society. The elaborate courtesy and deference are only substitutes for real respect.[16]

What is particularly significant is that Furstenberg calls into question the idyllic and nostalgic picture of domestic felicity that had been previously thought to apply to the family of that era. In spite of indications that "American women made dutiful and affectionate wives," there was also considerable evidence of "boredom and dissatisfaction" with their severely restricted role rights and numerous domestic duties.[17]

Yet in spite of dissatisfaction, boredom, and restiveness, divorce as a way out of the marital situation for women "did not take on great significance [in America] until after the Civil War." [18] Precisely because, prior to the advent of widespread industrialization in America, the woman could do little but remain in her status of "property," there was little divorce. But by no means does this show that before greatly expanded labor markets wives were "happier" with their lot. On the contrary, there is indication of discontent on the part of some wives, along with a state of powerlessness to utilize the safety-valve of divorce to modify their situation.

FIG. 2.1 CONTINUUM OF MARRIED FEMALE STATUSES IN RELATION TO HUSBANDS

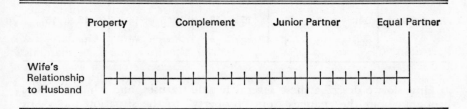

CHANGE AS AN OUTCOME OF CONFLICT

CHANGES IN THE STRUCTURE OF HUSBAND-WIFE RELATIONS

Figure 2.1 suggests a continuum of changes in female status definitions since the beginnings of the Feminist movement. We shall discuss specific definitions of these statuses shortly, but first it is well to note the ap-

16. Furstenberg, pp. 331ff.
17. *Ibid.*
18. *Ibid.*

proximate proportions of women found within the scope of each status category. Whereas in the late eighteenth century almost all married women were solely the property of the male, no Western woman today need *legally* be in that position. Voting, elective, and ambassadorial office, major legal rights, and so on—all are now formally open to women.

Nevertheless, the *actual* social position possessed by women both out of the family, and in it, remains subordinate to that of men. In terms of Figure 2.1 most married women today are probably found around the *complement* points of the continuum, and a minority in and around the *junior partner* segments. As we shall later define it, only a minute percentage would be found at the *equal partner* points.

FIG. 2.2   RATIO OF HUSBAND–WIFE RIGHTS AND DUTIES

		A Wife as Property		B Wife as Complement		C Wife as Junior Partner		D Wife as Equal Partner	
		H	W	H	W	H	W	H	W
Instrumental Roles:	Duties	15	15	15	12	15	9	15	15
	Rights	15	1	14	5	14	8	15	15
Expressive Roles:	Duties	2	15	15	15	15	15	15	15
	Rights	15	1	15	15	15	15	15	15

How do we describe these several female statuses, and what processes brought about the changes from "property" to the situation today? In Figure 2.2 the row labeled "instrumental" roles includes Murdock's description of the economic interdependence inherent within marriage. But it also includes power and decision-making behaviors within marriage, plus performance of necessary household tasks (child care, cooking, and so on). The row labeled "expressive" includes Murdock's notion of sexual behavior, plus the full range of primary interactions between husbands and wives (companionship, communication, understanding) which are commonly thought of as indicators of "marital satisfaction." Moreover, both the instrumental and expressive roles are subdivided into sets of duties and sets of rights.

Property

In the *A* section of Figure 2.2, the status of the wife is labeled *property*. The measurement of this status is based on the ratio of role rights and duties she possesses when compared to those of her husband. For instance, let us assign hypothetical numbers to the duties and rights segments of both the instrumental and expressive role dimensions for both husbands and wives. Let us arbitrarily assume a scale from 1 (low) to 15 (high). Looking first at the husband's instrumental role, we may say that while he ranked high (15) on duties to provide economically for his family, he also ranked high (15) on instrumental *rights*—i.e., household chores performed for him by his wife: cooking, cleaning, washing, bearing and caring for his children. Included among these rights was his wife's deference to his authority in whatever *he* considered to be critical areas of household policy and decision-making:

> . . . generally observers remarked that women deferred to their husbands' decisions in cases of disagreement.[19]

In contrast, at the instrumental dimension, the wife had numerous household duties (score of 15) to care for her husband and *his* children, while her rights (score of 1) were restricted to little more than ultimate protection from murder by her husband, whether by slow starvation or passionate outburst. In this regard, Mill makes the point that, so long as the wife was defined as property, if a husband mistreated her, "in no other case . . . is the person who has been proved judicially to have suffered an injury, replaced under the physical power of the culprit who inflicted it." [20]

At the expressive level of Figure 2.2*A*, the husband ranks high on rights to receive, for example, sexual gratification from his wife, and low on duties other than to provide minimal affection to his wife. The wife's expressive duties (to provide sexual gratifications) are great (score of 15), while her rights are virtually nonexistent (score of 1).

Complement

When we compare Figure 2.2*B* with *A*, we find that when the wife is defined as *complement*, her instrumental rights have increased slightly. At the expressive level, her rights have increased substantially, as have the husband's duties toward her. This kind of role structure is the one which has increasingly come to predominate in America since the Civil War and, more recently, in Western society as a whole.

19. Furstenberg, 1966, p. 336.
20. Mill, p. 443.

Whereas in the status of *property* she was often merely a chattel for the husband's sexual expression, as *complement* she gradually began to demand increasing levels of affectional satisfactions for herself. This was true, not only in terms of physical affection and sexual intimacies, but also in terms of companionship during leisure time, plus the capability to communicate with and to understand each other. She wanted to be, in short, something the wife historically had seldom, if ever, been defined as—*a friend to her husband*. These demands became part of the process of husband-wife bargaining and conflict, in the sense that wives were now seeking to establish these kinds of rights within marriage.

At the instrumental level, the definition of her economic status evolved from the right to mere *survival* (as property), to the right to a *comfortable living* (pre-World War II), to the right to *affluence* (post-1945). Alongside these stages of rising life-style expectations by the wife, was sought the right to contribute to the family's life style through her *own* employment. (Most wives who work can be placed somewhere in or around the junior partner points of the continuum shown in Figure 2.1.) Willingness to bargain and conflict with her husband over these rights meant that she began to gain a certain amount of family authority. She was no longer the totally powerless individual that she formerly had been.

Consequently, in Figure 2.2B, when we look at the wife as complement, we see definite increases in the quantitative level of rights she possesses compared with her former status as property. At the expressive level, for instance, the modern woman demands the same kinds and levels of emotional gratification from marriage that her husband does, and it is now his duty to supply these gratifications. With regard to the expressive role relations, therefore, it may be said with some accuracy that modern husbands and wives are on relatively equal ground. That is, they both demand and expect to get these kinds of gratifications from the other at about the same level of intensity (both sexes have rights and duties scores of 15). If anything, the wife as *complement* may expect a higher level of expressive rewards than the husband, owing to the fact that as *complement* marriage remains her central life interest.[21]

Nevertheless, at the instrumental level all available evidence demonstrates that the husband remains, in spite of what Mogey calls "a century of declining paternal authority," the dominant figure in the wife-as-complement situation.[22] When the wife's role is defined as complement —one in which the needs and interests of her husband and his occupation (plus the needs and interests of her children) are more important

21. Scanzoni, 1970.
22. Mogey, 1957.

than her own—she is going to have fewer instrumental rights, and more such duties than her husband. To be sure, there is a certain change in the husband-wife duties-rights ratio when she is defined as complement rather than property: she can demand a certain life style from her husband. She can expect him at times to share in particular household chores. She can try to disagree with him over certain matters and may sometimes get her way. At the same time, because her husband is chief family provider, he possesses more resources than she; hence, he retains more authority. And virtually every study shows that the better he provides (greater income, occupational status, education), the more authority he has.[23]

Junior Partner

Even when we look at Figure 2.2C, wife as junior partner, we see that her instrumental duties-rights ratio changes somewhat but not substantially. This status could be applied to the increasing numbers of married women who work outside the home. But the vast majority of these women do so as a sideline to their domestic duties, their main motive being to improve the family's life style. For example, wives are most likely to work when additional consumer goods are desired for the family, or when there are pressing financial needs.[24] It is not difficult, therefore, to explain census data which show that the greater the husband's annual income, the less likely the wife is to be employed.[25] Most wives of better-paid husbands apparently feel that they simply do not need to work. Moreover, for most white women who do work, the usual pattern is to be employed prior to the birth of the first child, then to quit, and *perhaps* to return to work as the last child grows older or leaves home. But even if she does return there is rarely the same commitment to work as is there for her husband.

Still we can label her (Figure 2.1) as being somewhat beyond complement and as a kind of *junior partner,* chiefly because there is evidence from several sources that the working wife has more family authority than her nonworking counterpart.[26] Her instrumental duties decline (score of 9) in the sense that she is less obliged to defer always and as much to her husband's wishes. Her instrumental rights increase (score of 8) in the sense of greater authority regarding family decisions. Because she too supplies resources to the family unit, she has greater bargaining power.

23. *See* Scanzoni, 1970, for a review of this literature.
24. Lebergott, 1960, pp. 388ff.
25. *Current Population Reports,* P–60, No. 64, pp. 1–3.
26. *See* Scanzoni, 1970, 1971, for discussion of this literature.

But because she does not occupy *the* provider role in the same sense as her husband (i.e., her job is not as critical to family survival), she still remains merely at the status of junior partner. This continued subordinate status can also be seen from those studies which show that when the wife works, she often continues to perform just as many household chores as wives who do not work.[27] Although not all studies confirm it, it appears that husbands of working wives do not significantly increase their participation in these chores; instead these wives simply add their work duties to their home chores.[28] Interestingly, some studies report that husbands of working wives in Sweden and in the Soviet Union seem just as reluctant as many American husbands to help in household chores.[29]

The explanation suggested here for these kinds of changes in structural patterns resulting in an increase in female role rights and a corresponding decrease in her role duties is that they came about as the result of long-term conflicts generated by wives to obtain a more favorable duties-rights ratio. Though not necessarily consciously nor rationally calculated, increasing numbers of wives evidently began to believe and accept many of the arguments and premises of the Feminists. Undergirded by the spreading ideology of individualism, and by increasing alternative opportunities outside the family (employment in particular), wives found themselves in a better bargaining position within marriage:

> . . . the new factory system transformed existing labor force patterns for women. By 1831, one of the founding fathers of Lowell (Mass.) could pridefully note that "no less than thirty-nine thousand females find employment in the cotton factories of the United States." Yet before "the establishment of these and other domestic manufactures this labor was almost without employment." [30]

We may assume that the logic (though sometimes unconscious) became "if women are able to vote (e.g., 1869 in Wyoming), own property, take paid employment, and have other legal rights, then she ought to have certain rights in bargaining with her husband." In this fashion, the notion of male-female as competing interest groups gradually filtered into marriage *qua institution* from the struggles and conflicts going on in the economic, religious, and political institutions. The conflicts that subsequently emerged within marriage resulted in a structural pattern

27. Goode, 1963, p. 63; Wilensky, p. 126.
28. Conflicting evidence on the American situation comes from Blood and Wolfe, and from Hoffman.
29. Dahlström and Liljeström, in Dahlström, pp. 30ff; Field, pp. 22ff.
30. Lebergott, 1960.

consisting of a more favorable arrangement of rights and duties than formerly, as represented by the changes in Figure 2.2.

The issue of why the early Feminists did not concentrate more *directly* on marriage and the family itself and make that particular institution an arena for specific struggles is a complex one. Either of the present predominant statuses (though more favorable to women than that of property) still subordinate them when compared to males in terms of role-rights and duties. Both the statuses of complement and junior partner are based on rather sharp sex-role differentiation (husband as provider, wife as expressive hub).

Historians of the nineteenth-century Feminist movement indicate different reasons for this relative lack of direct confrontation with the family institution, but one major reason seems to stand out. The early Feminists were very sensitive to the criticism (and perhaps believed it themselves) that to tamper in any way with the structure of the family was to invite immediate chaos into the whole of society.[31] Though never explicit as to just exactly how anarchy, disorder, and confusion would run rampant if family roles were altered, these were nevertheless widespread convictions in England and America at that time. Apparently, therefore, to avoid the accusation that they were undermining the very fabric of society, direct confrontations with traditional family patterns were avoided.

Kraditor, among others, claims that the failure to face those structural realities has perpetuated the long-standing inequalities between the sexes.[32] In chapters four and five, we shall look at how the present-day Neofeminists are facing these realities, and what this portends for future changes from *complement* and *junior partner* to the status of *equal partner*.

In trying to understand the dynamics of Figures 2.1 and 2.2, we must say that most wives today are complement or junior partner, or else some combination of the two. Her change in status from property to these current statuses came about as the result of her increasing capability to engage in conflict (to increase rights and decrease duties) with her husband. Hence, the key to understanding structural changes in marriage patterns over the last century lies with the ongoing conflict that has occurred between males and females *qua* interest groups. The alteration of role relationships has been a consequence of the increasing unwillingness of wives to remain at the property end of the continuum and their determination to move toward the partnership end.

Moreover, the fact that increasing numbers of women today (as a

31. O'Neill, 1969; Kraditor, p. 8.
32. *Ibid., passim.*

result of revived Feminism) are beginning to realize that they remain in statuses subordinate to men suggests that ongoing conflict between the sexes will probably continue (perhaps increase), and may make the present male-female instrumental rights-duties ratio still more favorable to females. Thus it is clear why the issue of male-female conflict is a theoretical tool for understanding historic and current changes in family structure and predicting the future structure of marriage.

CHANGES IN THE INCIDENCE OF DIVORCE

Male-female conflict also provides a way to understand the long-term increases in divorce described in chapter one. As we saw, dissolution rates have risen gradually but steadily throughout the United States and most of the Western World during the last century—the time when women have been pressing for greater rights and equality. In other words, the conflicts between female and male *qua* interest groups to change (or to retain) male prerogatives within the institution of the family has had increases in rates of marital dissolution as one of its *unintended* consequences.[33] As Mogey puts it, "as the legal and customary power of the father declined, so has the number of broken families increased." [34]

Hence, it is female "self-seeking," this effort to gain more rights and privileges, that *in part,* at least, lies behind the increasing cross-national rates of divorce. For when females seek personal rewards from marriage, they have at times come into conflict with the reward-seeking that males have traditionally carried on in marriage. The outcome of this clash, in comparison with earlier historical periods in which females were willingly subservient, must necessarily be a rise in marital tensions and dissolution.

The inexorable forces of an ever-expanding industrial economy are lined up against male maintenance of traditional sex roles, and on the side of women who wish to restructure their sex roles to enjoy in greater measure the benefits and rewards proffered by that kind of society:

> Men have fought a rear-guard action, winning this battle and losing that one, but in general retreating.[35]

While men today still maintain a dominant position vis-à-vis women, the struggle between them continues:

> Men typically exaggerate when they assert that women have achieved equal rights. It seems fair to say that women demand a greater range of *rights* than men are willing to concede, just as men are willing to impose a few more *obligations* than women are willing to accept. In a period of great

33. O'Neill, 1969, pp. 18–19.
34. Mogey, 1957, p. 235.
35. Goode, 1966, in Merton and Nisbet, p. 506.

change of sex roles, there is necessarily considerable tension in the day-to-day interaction of husbands and wives.[36]

The struggle for increased rights and privileges for women has become diffused through ever-widening segments of the population. Since there are more people now (especially women) who believe that they are not receiving all the rewards they feel they deserve (or that their marital rights-duties ratio is not favorable to them), there is obviously greater likelihood of marital dissolution in 1970 than there was in 1920, or in 1920 than there was in 1900, and so forth.

> . . . the existence of tensions in sex roles means that there are bound to be more conflicts between husbands and wives now than a hundred years ago; . . . it cannot be surprising that the likelihood of divorce is greater than a century ago.[37]

The fact that divorce rates are increasing in many societies indicates that male-female conflict is a phenomenon linked with worldwide modernization and not specifically with the United States alone. Recall too from the prior chapter the attempt in the USSR to *impose* sexual equality on the population and the consequences of that policy for that nation's divorce rate.

> These pressures and patterns are not at all peculiar to the United States. . . . Rather, the United States is the vanguard of a process which is becoming worldwide. [Other] countries follow behind simply because they are going through similar phases at a later date.[38]

Values and Beliefs and the Willingness to Divorce

It would seem, therefore, that throughout the world married women are ever less willing to have their rights ignored, and ever more willing to contest the ancient prerogatives of males. The ideology of individualism implies a "pragmatic" view of marriage. In simple terms, this means that personal rights ultimately exceed loyalty to the (family) group.

Across the world, increasing numbers of women (and men) are adopting this orientation instead of the traditional belief in the intrinsic *permanence* of marriage. To believe in the inherent permanence of marriage is to believe it to be a lifelong contract, binding on both partners, that should not be dissolved no matter how punishing the situation. This is not to say that prior to this era of history no one ever viewed marriage in pragmatic fashion. As early as 1643, the Puritan apologist John Milton argued for it in quite elegant prose:

36. *Ibid.*
37. *Ibid.*
38. *Ibid.*

> Lest therefore so noble a creature as man should be shut up incurably under a worse evil by an easy mistake . . . the mercy of this mosaic law (divorcement) was graciously exhibited.[39]

But do persons in modern society conceive of marriage in *totally* pragmatic terms? Do permanence-type values figure in at all? In a study comparing a sample of persons from dissolved marriages with those from existing marriages, an attempt was made to develop an index of pragmatism and a separate index of permanence.[40] The two opinion questions in the former index were:

1. If a husband and wife simply cannot get along, it is probably better for them to end their marriage.

2. It is proper for a couple to feel that if their marriage does not work out, they can always obtain a divorce.

For the index of permanence, the opinion questions were:

1. Divorce is wrong except for adultery.

2. Marriage is for life even if the couple is unhappy.

Persons from dissolved marriages scored significantly higher (statistically) than those from existing marriages on the *pragmatism* index.[41] But did divorced persons hold these values prior to their divorce experiences, or did they come to adopt them as a result of the unusually traumatic events surrounding marital dissolution? We cannot say for certain, but the concomitant finding was that there was no significant difference between the two samples with regard to *permanence-type* values.[42] These data lead us to suggest the hypothesis that most American (perhaps Western) couples cling to *both* types of values with virtually equal strength, in *seemingly paradoxical fashion*. We could assume that persons begin marriage holding to the ideal of permanence, but at the same time, in the back of their minds they also hold the notion of pragmatism.

There is nothing unusual about persons simultaneously holding contrasting or paradoxical sets of values and beliefs. It is erroneous, however, to assume that values influence behavior apart from the structural situation in which the person finds himself. In marriage, this means situations where punishments and rewards are balanced in some type of

39. Milton, 1963.
40. Scanzoni, 1968.
41. Persons from dissolved marriages (N = 110), $\bar{x}$ = 6.52 on Pragmatism Index; persons from existing marriages (N = 160), $\bar{x}$ = 5.86; t = 3.8 (p < .01).
42. Persons from dissolved marriages, Permanence Index, $\bar{x}$ = 6.05; Existing Marriages, $\bar{x}$ = 6.19; n.s.

ratio. Most Americans very likely enter marriage hoping that the rewards will outweigh the costs and that their unions will be permanent. Since the overwhelming majority of unions are not dissolved, we may assume that the reward-cost ratio is defined as relatively favorable.[43] Nonetheless, it may not be said that their permanence values "caused" marital stability, because it is assumed that they hold pragmatic values with virtually equal intensity. Since neither set of opposite values can therefore be primarily responsible for stability, then it must be the result of something else—i.e., the internal marital situation, or the reward-cost ratio.

Accordingly, among those who divorce, pragmatic values cannot be said to "cause" dissolution; instead the basic influence is likely to be internal and external factors (role alternatives open to the female) associated with the marriage. Are values then irrelevant in explaining stability-instability? No, but more research is needed as to their actual significance. Among Catholics, Conservative Protestants, Orthodox Jews, or Black Muslims, for instance, theological convictions may reinforce permanence-type values and lead certain persons to endure far more punishing situations than would persons who do not share those particular convictions. Likewise, if it could be shown that Americans were completely sloughing off permanence values and no longer holding them as a kind of balance to pragmatic values, then one might predict a rise in overall rates of marital instability. That is, being significantly more pragmatic than "permanent," persons might be less willing to endure the kinds of punishing situations that otherwise would have been tolerated in earlier years. Therefore, the place of values in explaining or predicting behavior (in this case, marital stability) lies, in part, in the way in which they do, or do not, aid persons to evaluate their own ongoing marital situations or reward-cost ratios.

CONCLUSION

In this chapter our chief concern has been to dispel the misconception that the conjugal marital pattern has been static and that unique forces have suddenly appeared on the scene to bring about radical and profound change. Instead, we have seen that the closest equivalent to an authentically "static" period of marital structure was prior to the nineteenth century, when males had effectively engulfed females in a state of coercion and subjugation.

Certain events in the larger society then crystallized a sense of "class-consciousness" and "oppression" among some females. And while marital

---

43. This ratio is described more fully toward the close of chapter four.

structure itself was not directly confronted by the early Feminists, the byproducts of their struggles and conflicts gradually filtered in *ad hoc* fashion into the institution of marriage. From the perspective of continuing male-female conflict, we have seen how and why marital role structure has changed, and how these changes are, in turn, responsible for increases in the worldwide incidence of divorce. The changes in marital patterns have consisted, for wives, of an increasingly favorable, and for husbands an increasingly less favorable, ratio of rights and privileges to duties and obligations.

III. The Motivation to Marry

In chapter one we saw that while there have been long-term changes in the frequency with which marital dissolution occurs, there is no indication that marriage itself is in a state of disintegration. At the same time, in the previous chapter, we saw that the marital relationship in Western society has not been static. It has experienced a process of long-term change, and change in the structure of the relationship lies at the heart of the increasing frequency with which some persons end it. In this chapter, we turn to the question of the motivation to marry.

We shall look first at the very different kinds of socialization experiences to which most boys and girls in Western society are exposed. Next, we shall consider love as a form of social exchange in which the partners operate in terms of what they learned during their earlier socialization. Marriage, it will be seen, is simply an extension of the kinds of reciprocities begun during the premarital love relationship. We then discuss "trial marriage" as an attempt on the part of some to introduce some rationality into these processes, and finally we close the chapter by looking at some data which suggest that in spite of the considerable range of non-rational elements involved, marriage does not yet appear to be on the threshold of obsolescence.

DIVERGENT SOCIALIZATION OF MALES AND FEMALES

Beginning in the nursery and continuing throughout their years of maturation, children encounter very different types of socialization experiences depending on the accident of their sex. Most sociologists without dismissing the existence of genetic predispositions, are more concerned with the social conditions that lead to "sex-typing." By sex-typing Sears refers to certain cultural behaviors which are taught to one or the other sex and which are subsequently enacted by that sex. For example:

> One of the significant areas in which sharp sex differences are found is in the expression of aggression. Among adults, men commit more homicides, more suicides, and are arrested more frequently for assault and battery. In adolescence, male deliquency is far more frequently aggressive than is female delinquency. These sex differences extend downward in the age scale at least to the age of three years.[1]

To try to explain these differences, Sears reports a study of young children and their mothers in which he found that mothers reacted very differently to the expression of aggression by boys compared to girls.[2] Girls were much more restricted than boys in showing aggressive behavior toward neighborhood children or parents. Likewise, boys were encouraged to fight back when attacked, girls were not. Boys predominantly received physical punishment, and most often from their fathers. The major disciplinarians of girls were their mothers, and they used withdrawal of love—a psychological rather than a physical means—to obtain control.

In short, many studies reveal that from their earliest years, males in our society are socialized to adopt aggressive, active, forceful behaviors. Females, conversely, are socialized to accept passivity, conformity, and "goodness of conduct." Komarovsky underscores the point that teaching the feminine role may be quite unconscious to the parent; and the child may be equally unaware that a particular role is being learned.[3]

Since, as Freud and others have argued, "the whole essence of femininity lies in repressing aggressiveness," [4] it is clear how her socialization and her femininity prepare the woman to step into the role of complement to the male, i.e., as the expressive hub of the conjugal family. We suggest that the more completely a woman accepts this type of role, the less likely she is to generate *certain* kinds of serious conflict with her husband that might eventually result in marital dissolution. This is simply because the "good wife" has learned to fit the man's needs, and to meet his wishes and demands—especially those which arise in conjunction with his occupational role. Most females are not socialized to be an *individual* (especially an individual achiever) in the same sense that the male is. For the male, individualistic occupational achievement

1. Sears, p. 133.
2. *Ibid.*, pp. 136–37.
3. Komarovsky, 1953, p. 54.
4. Horner, p. 56.

becomes the main channel whereby he is legitimately permitted to express learned aggressiveness. For the woman, as Rossi puts it: "From Bill's daughter to John's wife to Johnny's mother and Bill's grandmother catches the broad sweep of many a woman's life span." [5]

But at the same time that families socialize their girls in the traditional orientations described above, they have been increasingly exposing them to more modern, individualistic orientations. These usually take the form of pressures to do well in school, and these pressures are, of course, reinforced by the school system itself.

At the same time that parents, teachers, and peers hold up traditional ideals for girls to emulate, they also extend modern values in terms of individualistic academic and occupational achievements. Nonetheless, for most young women pressures toward the traditional still tend to outweigh pressures toward modern role conceptions.

A recent study of a nationwide sample of college women showed that only some 20 percent of the women could be classified as "modern," or in the investigator's terminology, "unconventional." [6] Unconventionality was measured by the kind of occupation the women wanted to enter following college. Those women who wanted to enter male occupations such as medicine, law, and business, were classified as "unconventional." As predicted by the researcher these tended mostly to be women from higher status backgrounds. But student aspiration is one thing, actually achieving one's goal is quite another, especially for women. As a result of intense pressures on women to conform to traditional expectations, other studies suggest that five years after college a good number of that unconventional 20 percent might not be so unconventional after all.[7]

LOVE AND REWARD-SEEKING

The initial point to keep in mind, therefore, in trying to probe the question of why people marry is the very different kinds of socialization that girls encounter when compared to boys. In a moment we shall make explicit some of the consequences of this divergent socialization for marriage. But before we can do that, we need to explore what is meant by "love." Blau suggests that "love is the polar case of intrinsic attraction." [8] By "intrinsic attraction" he means a relationship that is considered an "end in itself," as contrasted with an *extrinsic* (or secondary) relationship in which the relationship is considered merely a means to ends beyond

5. Rossi, 1969, p. 2.
6. Walshok, 1969.
7. *See* chapter five, "Rapidity and Extensiveness of Change," for a review of literature pertinent to this question.
8. Blau, p. 76.

the relationship itself.[9] For example, in a secondary relationship, a sales-man takes a client golfing, but the "golfing relationship" serves *chiefly* as a means to sell a service or product. In an intrinsic relationship, it is sufficient for friends or lovers to be together, and simply to enjoy the other person for his own sake.

> Love appears to make human beings unselfish, since they themselves enjoy giving pleasure to those they love, but this selfless devotion generally rests on an interest in maintaining the other's love.[10]

Love is generally conceived of in altruistic terms, but "even a mother's devotion to her children is rarely entirely devoid of the desire to main-tain their attachment to her. *Exchange processes occur in love relations as well as in [extrinsic] social associations*" [11] (italics supplied). In chapter two references were made to "reward-seeking" carried on by both hus-bands and wives. Male-female reward-seeking from each other begins prior to marriage at the very outset of their love relationship. The pros-pect of certain rewards from the other is what forms the basis of their relationship in the first place, but in order to receive those rewards each must in turn provide the kinds of rewards expected by the other. To be sure, rewards are furnished "to express and confirm his own commitment and to promote the other's growing commitment to the association." [12] This ongoing process is labeled "social exchange" and is the basis for the formation and *maintenance* of *any* social relationship including love and marriage:

> A man falls in love if the attractiveness of a woman has become unique in his eyes. . . . His attraction to her makes him dependent on her for important rewards and anxious to impress and please her to arouse a reciprocal affection that would assure him these rewards. . . . Human beings evidently derive pleasure from doing things for those they love. . . . The repeated experience of being rewarded by the increased attachment of a loved one after having done a variety of things to please him may have the effect that giving pleasure to loved ones becomes intrinsically gratifying.[13]

If a love relationship is "to develop into a lasting mutual attachment," then the "lovers' affection for and commitment to one another [must] expand at roughly the same pace." [14] That is, if one lover makes sig-nificantly greater inputs than the other into the relationship, this "in-

9. *Ibid.,* pp. 35–36.
10. *Ibid.,* p. 76.
11. *Ibid.*
12. *Ibid.*
13. *Ibid.,* pp. 76–77.
14. *Ibid.,* pp. 84–85.

vites exploitation or provokes feelings of entrapment, both of which obliterate love. . . . The weak interest of the less committed or the frustrations of the more committed probably will sooner or later prompt one or the other to terminate it." [15] Hence, if both parties define their inputs and rewards as "just," "beneficial," or "satisfactory," then the love relationship is quite likely to be maintained and to evolve into marriage. If one party does not feel that the cost-reward ratio is satisfactory to him, he (she) may cut back his inputs, thereby reducing the satisfactions of the other, and thus increasing the likelihood that the relationship will be terminated.

It is a general sociological principle that associations are formed and maintained on the basis of reciprocity—exchanged rewards and benefits. A love relationship is no exception. To be sure, since it is primarily an *intrinsic* relationship, persons are not overtly being "used" as means to extrinsic ends. But to conceive of love and marriage as purely altruistic is to miss the point that rarely, if ever, can human love be sustained unless it be requited. And although later we shall say more about common values and shared interests of a married couple, to posit value consensus or common interests as the prime basis for love and marriage exhibits only a tiny fraction of the iceberg, and totally misses the dynamics of marriage formation and subsequent interaction.

Jessie Bernard has tried to apply some of the ideas of game theory to marriage, and obviously one of the central notions of game theory is the seeking of individual rewards and interests.[16] As long as players find the game rewarding, they will continue in it, and drop out when it ceases to reward them. The individual reward-seeking is in no way inimical to the relationship. Indeed the more each feels rewarded the more solid it becomes.

Thus, there is no foundation for the assumption that individual interests and group interests are necessarily mutually exclusive or contradictory. Moreover, it is naïve to think that love and marriage relationships could be maintained unless individual gratifications were satisfied.

DECISIONS SURROUNDING MARRIAGE

Thus far in exploring the motivation to marry we have said that we must take into account divergent socialization by sex, and that a love relationship is a particular case of social exchange. It is now time to tie these notions together and to connect them to decisions to actually marry.

Prior to the last century-and-a-half, most marriages in most parts of

15. *Ibid.,* p. 84.
16. Bernard, 1964.

the world were not based on decisions reached by only two persons after a love relationship such as that just described. Marriages were arranged by older members of the larger kin or line. Some anthropologists and sociologists have employed notions of social exchange, bargaining, and reciprocity to help explain how arranged marriages were formed:

> Significant economic interests are usually involved, both in the exchange of goods that accompanies the marriage and in the effect of marriage on the dispersal or concentration of inherited property, wealth, and resources.[17]

But as western societies began to modernize, the power of the kin to control social and economic rewards and resources declined. Correspondingly, its capability to control mate selection declined and the power of the prospective partners to select their own mates increased. With modernization, therefore, comes greater participation of prospective partners in the processes of bargaining and exchange that precede their own marriages. The ideal of love, rather than conformity to the kin, has become the manifest basis for mate selection:

> People, it is said, marry for love. If this is the case, love is a pious force yoked to propriety. People have a curious tendency to fall in love with those who are socially suitable.[18]

SOCIALIZATION AND LOVE

The point made by these researchers is that persons today bring with them into the love relationship the consequences of their earlier background experiences—in particular, socialization into *disparate* sex roles:

> The stress on romantic love, however, reveals that they are not conscious of the values that guide their choices. These values define good and bad marriages, and are to a considerable extent built into the dating process itself. The qualities that boys and girls seek in each other are predictive of those they will seek in marriage. Girls generally boast of the social skills and status characteristics of their dates—their dancing, their cars, and the places they went. Boys boast of the physical appearance, social skills, and cooperativeness of the girls. Later, when they marry, girls are said to make a good marriage when they marry a successful or up-and-coming man, boys when they marry a beautiful, charming, and faithful girl. To some degree then, the attributes of a successful marriage (from the girl's viewpoint) can be translated into social status. A marriage is successful when a girl marries a man of higher social status than herself.[19]

17. Zelditch, 1964, pp. 686–87.
18. Westley and Epstein, p. 158.
19. *Ibid.*, pp. 158–59.

While there has been a significant change in the locus of control of mate selection, there has been no change in its basic objective, i.e., *to try to strike the "best bargain" possible*. But the nature of the bargain has changed considerably, as graphically portrayed by Figures 2.1 and 2.2. The above quote describes vividly the content of male-female sex roles when the female holds the status of complement, or junior partner. During the premarital love period women provide the rewards of physical appearance, social skills, and cooperativeness. Once married, most women continue to supply the expressive, supportive, and nurturant benefits of beauty, charm, and fidelity. In *exchange* they expect from men, and receive prior to marriage, certain types of social skills and status characteristics. Subsequent to marriage the rewards they expect are bound up in notions of his being at least a "good provider," but more desirably, "a successful or up-and-coming man."

These specialized roles were the roles learned in childhood by most persons in Western society, and are the result of the socialization experiences described earlier. Moreover, certain constraints operate so that persons tend to marry other persons from the same race, and with similar education, and to a lesser extent than formerly, similar social class background, and also religion. Persons perceive that the "best" kinds of bargains can generally be struck with persons most like them in these critical social categories.

However, with the passing of control from the kin to the partners, there is a change in the degree of *permanence* of the arrangement. The exchange of benefits between kin groups sealed the marriage and served as a binding force on a lifetime contract. But currently because individuals, rather than kin, are primarily responsible for the bargaining processes, there is no once-and-for-all exchange to inevitably seal a lifetime contract. Instead, what *is* lifelong is the notion of an ongoing quest or seeking for rewards, or the best bargain possible. Therefore, persons today bargain during courtship, during the decision to marry, and furthermore *they continue this bargaining on through the length of their marriage*.

In describing these kinds of changes, McCall conceptualizes modern marriage not as a contract at all, but as a "restrictive trade agreement":

> The two individuals agree to exchange only with one another, at least until such time as the balance of trade becomes unfavorable in terms of broader market considerations. They agree to exchange exclusively for so long as the rewards in *this* involvement exceed the costs of continuing it in the face of chances for other rewards elsewhere.[20]

McCall's conceptualization may be overdrawn in that, as we saw in the prior chapter, there is evidence that persons would ideally prefer their

20. McCall, pp. 197–98.

marriage to be a permanent arrangement, while there is none to sub-
stantiate the notion that people prefer dissolution to stability.[21]

However, McCall's main point is that dissolution is considered more
desirable than an untenable (i.e., unjust, unfair) set of ongoing bargaining processes. And in this critical notion she appears to be correct. For
this reason we cannot understand the nature of marriage and its dissolution in modern society without also grasping the essence of our courtship
system. Males and females socialized into their differing roles *prior* to
marriage seek the different kinds of rewards from each other that they
have learned are appropriate to these roles; they enter marriage because
they perceive it will continue to supply these particular rewards and
gratifications; they remain in the relationship so long as expected rewards
are forthcoming; they withdraw from it if rewards diminish below and
costs exceed desired expectations.

These realities of courtship and marriage tend to be clouded (especially for the never-married) by the romantic love complex, which dictates
that prospective partners are not supposed to weigh *reward* elements, at
least consciously. Nonrational, romantic, person-centered considerations
are supposed to be paramount—lesser elements are too crass to be included. Romantic love thus obscures the premarital bargaining process
and places some persons in a situation which may eventually work to
their detriment. Not that suppressing the reality of the process makes it
disappear either before or after marriage. It is present whether recognized
or not, though there is greater probability that the daily pressures of
marriage make it more evident subsequent, rather than prior to, the
union, when passionate love may indeed have been a blinding force.

TRIAL MARRIAGE

Although chapter five will be devoted specifically to projected changes
in family forms, some attention to trial or "experimental" marriage is
relevant here because of our discussion of rationality in the selection of
marriage partners. Recall that marriage exists when two or more persons
share expressive and economic interdependencies. By this definition persons who have an ongoing, covert, sexual liaison and who dwell in separate households would not be classified as married. But if two persons
share the same household, maintain expressive relations including sexual
access, and have their present socioeconomic state and future destinies
intertwined for a time—then by our definition they would be classified
as married. Implicit in this kind of arrangement is overtness. In most
settings it is very difficult to keep this situation a secret. Those who
attempt to maintain secrecy imply a weaker commitment to their mar-

21. Scanzoni, 1968; Hobart, 1963.

riage, or "restrictive trade agreement." If there are no efforts to shield the arrangement, it is genuinely a marriage in the sociological sense that two persons have publicly declared their intention to maintain these interdependencies.

Social, not legal, support is requisite to enter into marriage. However in a complex society, legal sanctions function as protection mechanisms. Adults are thereby relatively protected from undisclosed economic entanglements as a result of any former marriages by their partner, and from exploitation in their present one. Required tests for venereal diseases are designed to protect the physical well-being of both adults and any children. Likewise, legal sanctions provide a means for guarding the social and economic rights of children.

The critical point to keep before us now, however, is that trial marriage is basically an effort to introduce an element of explicit rationality into the love relationship. There are some adults in our society who argue that our legal system should provide for people to try out marriage for a brief, specified period, and then simply allow them to cease the arrangement whenever they desire.[22] Some younger people might prefer trial marriage because they may not be sure about the other person, and a trial would provide an opportunity to find out one way or the other. Others may simply wish to find out if they themselves are actually prepared to take on all the commitments of a legal marriage. Still others, on idealistic grounds, feel that legal marriage, with its seemingly binding features, can become a sham because "love may flee" yet the marriage be forced to continue. They feel that legal controls over marriage and divorce should be minimized and choices left entirely to the persons involved.

While in some respects they differ, all these varying viewpoints share the idea that persons in the midst of a love relationship are likely to strike a bargain they may later regret. To ameliorate the possibility of a seriously unfavorable cost-reward ratio from emerging, spokesmen for these viewpoints suggest a trial period (not legally binding) in which processes and outcomes of marital reciprocity and exchange can be weighed in terms of the daily routine of life together, and in a somewhat more dispassionate fashion than is usually possible during the usual premarital love relationship.

MARRIAGE RATES AND THE OBSOLESCENCE OF MARRIAGE

These varied spokesmen differ over what should follow the trial period. Some persons feel that if the trial is satisfactory (in terms of benefits and

---

22. Mead, 1970. Her essay first appeared in *Redbook* (July, 1966). Later, in the April, 1968, issue, after many readers objected, Mead seemed to hedge on her original formulations.

rewards exchanged) then it is legitimate, desirable, and useful to obtain legal sanctions for the marriage.[23] Others feel that legal sanctions are obsolete, unnecessary, and passé, and therefore need never be sought. So that when certain spokesmen allege that traditional marriage patterns are becoming irrelevant, one idea they have in mind is that persons are *permanently* bypassing the legal formalities and simply living together without ever seeking legal sanctions.

But is legal marriage actually becoming obsolete? The fact that conjugal marriage is not experiencing widespread disintegration or collapse should make us somewhat skeptical of that allegation, since many social critics tend to correlate disintegration with obsolescence.

Since 1890 the percentage of all men and women over fourteen years of age who never *legally* marry (and are therefore classed as "single") has steadily declined. In 1890, 32 percent of all such men were single; by 1960 it was 25 percent; and in 1969 it was 23.7 percent.[24] Twenty-seven percent of black males were single in 1969, compared to 23 percent of white males. In 1890 24 percent of all women over fourteen were single; by 1969, 19 percent of white women and 21 percent of black women were single.

Hence the percentage of all men and women who obtain a marriage license has steadily increased along with the great increase over the past eighty years in the absolute numbers of American men and women.

It is important to remember that the above figures include adolescents as young as fourteen, far below the 1969 median (average) age for first marriage (females = 20.8 yrs.; males = 23.2). The fact is that by age thirty-nine, only 5 percent of females, and 8 percent of males, have never legally married.[25] Thus long-term trends in the United States have been toward greater percentages of people legally married and fewer staying officially single.[26] "The basic fact . . . was that marriage was more nearly

---

23. Mead, 1970.
24. *Current Population Reports*, P–20, No. 198.
25. *Current Population Reports*, P–20, No. 198, pp. 12–13, for nonfarm population.
26. As we went to press, the Census Bureau released figures showing that the percent single of men and women *under 35* had increased in 1971 compared to those who were single and under 35 in 1960. For persons over 35, the long-term trend of decreasing singleness continued. The authors of the report warn, however, that the trend reversal among those under 35 is too recent to be evaluated in valid fashion. That is, we must wait several years "to determine whether or not (1) people are delaying marriage for a certain number of years, but still eventually marry in similar or greater proportions than before, or (2) people are simply not going to marry regardless of age, or (3) this is a cyclical phenomenon which will eventually alternate with a pattern of more people marrying at younger ages than is now the case." *Current Population Reports*. P–20, No. 225, p. 1.

the universal conjugal state among adult Americans of the 1960s than it had ever been before." [27]

There are no reliable data to indicate how many Americans are living together prior to legal union in some kind of trial arrangement of their own devising. (While there are data on the incidence of premarital intercourse among engaged and nonengaged persons, this behavior is not to be equated with genuine trial marriage as defined above.) Hence, we simply do not know how widespread that trend may be up to now. But however widespread it is, most persons whether having had a trial or not do seem eventually to seek legal sanctions for their marriage to each other or to someone else. In essence, legal marriage gives no indication of becoming obsolete or passé.

RATES AND PROBABILITIES OF REMARRIAGE AMONG THE DIVORCED

Another set of data that speak to the issue of the alleged decline of marriage is the behavior of those who have been divorced at least once. Since they have been "in" marriage as a husband or wife, they would seem best able to compare being "in" or "out" and to decide whether or not to enter marriage again. Their behavior should supply additional clues to any fundamental trends suggesting disillusionment with legal marriage as we know it.

In 1960, for example, the marriage rate among divorced men was 171 per 1,000 divorced men. Among single men, the rate was much lower, 72 per 1,000 single men.[28] Thus, divorced men appear to be more eager to re-enter marriage than single men are to enter it for the first time. This is even more strikingly evident among men in the 14 to 24 age bracket. There the marriage rate among divorced men is 367 per 1,000; among single men only 72 per 1,000. At every age interval, in fact, divorced men are substantially more likely to marry than are never married men.

The same generalizations apply to women. The overall 1960 marriage rate for divorced women was 124 per 1,000 divorced women; for single women, it was 90 per 1,000 single women. In the 14 to 24 age bracket the rates were 442 and 112, respectively; throughout the life cycle the rates of marriage for divorced women remain substantially higher than those for single women.

Further indication that behavior of the divorced signals no widespread disillusionment with nor repudiation of marriage can be seen when we compare the average annual chances of remarriage of the divorced in the

27. Carter and Glick, 1970, pp. 62–63.
28. Plateris, 1970, p. 10.

1960s with the 1950s.[29] Overall, in the fifties the chances of a divorced man remarrying were 125 out of every 1,000 divorced men; for a divorced woman the chances were 106 out of every 1,000 divorced women. In the sixties, these chances *rose* to 180 and 139 respectively. It remains true that the longer one remains divorced the fewer the chances of remarriage; but for both sexes in virtually every year of being divorced, the chances for remarriage went up in the sixties as compared to the fifties. Especially large during the sixties were the remarriage chances for those in the *first* year of divorce: fully a quarter (250) for women, nearly a third (318) for men. In the fifties, the chances for remarriage during the first year of divorce were only 206 per 1,000 for men and 164 per 1,000 for women.

It has been observed for some time that the stigma once attached to divorce is disappearing in Western society. These data would suggest that the additional stigma of *remarriage* is also beginning to disappear. We should expect these trends to continue into the seventies—i.e., increasing rates of remarriage of the divorced. Therefore, these kinds of behaviors also tend to undercut the notion of gradual "disappearance" of monogamous marriage, insofar as an increasing proportion of the population is concerned. Some persons may be indeed moving away from prevalent marriage forms, but they seem to be only marginally represented among those who have once "tried" marriage. Such persons, when they become dissatisfied with particular marital situations, "want out" and "get out" of those situations. But they appear to have some degree of hope that a *different* specific situation within the *same* general pattern will prove satisfactory, and their reentry into this pattern serves to affirm its legitimacy.

SERIAL MONOGAMY: FREQUENCY OF REPEATED MARRIAGE
AMONG THE DIVORCED

Reference was made in chapter one to the absence of any evidence for "serial monogamy" among the vast majority of the population, since most persons remain married to one spouse for most of their lives. However, the possibility exists that the minority of persons who are divorced may constitute a subgroup among whom serial monogamy has become legitimized. That is, they may be the ones who are most likely to shift rather frequently from spouse to spouse. The evidence, however, is contrary to any image of widespread mate-hopping even among the divorced. Government data indicate that approximately 75 percent of all Americans who obtain divorces each year are ending their *first* marriage. Around 20 percent of those getting divorced are ending a *second* marriage.[30] Only a

29. Current Population Reports, P–23, No. 32 (July 29, 1970).
30. Carter and Glick, 1970, p. 230; Plateris, 1969, p. 38.

tiny fraction of persons who divorce each year are ending a third marriage, and the proportion of those ending a fourth (or more) marriage is infinitesimal.[31] In 1967, of all white men under 70 years old who had been married 20 years or more, 82 percent had been married once, 16 percent had been married twice, and only 2 percent had been married 3 or more times. For black men the figures are 65, 30, and 5 percent respectively. For white women, the figures are 80, 18, and 2 percent; for black women 67, 29, and 4 percent.[32] Indeed, Glick and Norton challenge the widespread notion that second marriages tend to be less stable than first marriages by pointing out that the probability of divorce after the first marriage (6 per year per 1,000 men) is as large as the probability of divorce after the second marriage (5 per 1,000).

How then shall we define "serial monogamy"? The great majority of persons who divorce each year are ending their *first* legal marriage. Many of these legally remarry and most of them stay married. One would be stretching the point to define this behavior as serial monogamy. Since most divorces happen to those who marry relatively young and who are economically less well-off, it could be argued that their first marriages were hasty or ill-advised, and that the partners did not see beyond the constraints of "romantic love" toward the full range of economic and other realities involved in marriage. The second time around, it is likely they make a more rational choice of spouse.

On the other hand, it might be more justifiable to label the small minority of divorced persons who marry *more than twice* as displaying serial monogamy. Either they repeatedly make poor choices, or else for personality reasons they are unable to participate satisfactorily in the processes of reciprocity and conflict that maintain modern marriage. Even in these instances, however, we would have to determine if they normatively *prefer* serial monogamy to permanent monogamy, or whether it is merely the recurrence of punishing situations that induces their marital mobility.

CONCLUSION

In this chapter we have been concerned with the conditions that surround the formation of marriage. We saw that childhood socialization is related to the kind of reward-seeking that most males and females carry on with each other during the love relationship period. Processes of social exchange are clearly established during the love relationship, and become the basis for the bargain to be struck, i.e., the eventual decision to marry.

31. *Ibid.*
32. Glick and Norton, p. 313.

While we cannot be certain of the actual incidence of trial marriage in the United States, it is clear that legal conjugal unions have become increasingly prevalent over the past eighty years. Marriage behavior of the divorced also supports the notion of the continued prevalence of legal unions, and undercuts the notion of any widespread current trends toward serial monogamy.

There are several points that carry over into the following chapters. First, whether the marriage be legal or not, the processes of social exchange which emanate from childhood socialization, and which are carried out during the love relationship, continue right on into the marriage. There is no "magical transformation" that occurs simply because of a wedding ceremony or some other equivalent mechanism. Once we grasp the reality of reward-seeking as an intrinsic and inevitable mechanism within marriage, we are then prepared to examine in detail how reward-seeking *binds* or *dissolves* marriage, and also how it is at the root of *changes* in future marriage patterns.

IV. Marital Conflict as a Positive Force

Many people have a common-sense image of the "optimum" or "ideal" or "happy" family situation. Sprey labels this the "consensus-stable equilibrium approach" in which husbands and wives are said to share common values and interests. In this view conflict is usually thought to exclude consensus and is generally pictured as an aberrant phenomenon—pathological, negative, bad. Built into this perspective is a bias toward the desirability of equilibrium, adjustment, and *maintenance* of the marriage relationship. Seldom is the possibility considered that marital stability itself is a scientifically neutral question.

Even as a policy question it seems clear that not all couples should remain married. Therefore, in trying to understand the dynamics of husband-wife interaction, the first step would be to divest ourselves of the notion that equilibrium or stability for all is a necessary ideal—that *all* marriages could or should remain intact. Some adults and children may experience less trauma through dissolution than through stability.

A second and related step would be to rid ourselves of the idea that conflict is *ipso facto* bad or unhealthy within marriage. Sprey goes so far as to say that we ought to reject the consensus approach, because "the most fruitful theoretical approach toward the study of the family and its process is the use of a conflict framework. . . ."[1] However, Sprey errs in reaction to the error he is trying to correct, which was to ignore the place of conflict in marital interaction. It is corrected by showing how *both* consensus and conflict are inevitable and intrinsic parts of marital structure, not by dismissing the idea of consensus entirely. Coser remarks that:

1. Sprey, p. 700.

". . . conflict theory or integration theory [are not] rival explanatory systems. . . ." [2]

Actually, when Sprey defines his position more clearly the notion of consensus is not absent from his thinking. For him marital consensus is a kind of "negotiated order" which is nevertheless open to a process of continuous renegotiation. The question then becomes, how do we analyze the processes of negotiation which in the great majority of marriages result in an ongoing order or stability, yet which in others result in instability?

RECIPROCITY AND EXCHANGE IN MARRIAGE

Even though men and women may be described as interest groups in conflict, it would be a mistake to think of every individual female as being in conflict with every individual male. What we may say is that every husband and wife are bound together in processes of reciprocity that do at certain times evolve into conflict processes, which in turn may or may not be resolved.

Marital Role Reciprocity

We saw in chapter three that the reward-seeking begun during the love relationship continues on into the marital relationship.[3] It was also noted that a love relationship is basically an *intrinsic* relationship in that the relationship itself is deemed to be more significant than rewards *extrinsic* to it. Nevertheless, we also saw that certain features that might be labeled as extrinsic have been, up to this point in time, very much a part of the love relationship in modern society. Most males have supplied certain material and status rewards to females, while most females have supplied charm, physical beauty, nurturance, and support. Figure 4.1 is an expanded and more detailed version of figures 2.2B and 2.2C.[4] To understand the figure we must note Gouldner's comment that the concept of reciprocity "provides new leverage for analysis of the central problems of sociological theory, namely, accounting for stability and instability in social systems." [5]

How then does reciprocity help explain the stability of the social system of marriage? First, "reciprocity has its significance for *role* systems in that it tends to structure *each* role so as to include both rights and duties." [6]

---

2. Coser, 1967, pp. 8–9.
3. Turner, 1970, makes the same point, p. 43.
4. The following discussion is based on Scanzoni, 1970, pp. 17–21.
5. Gouldner, 1960, p. 162.
6. *Ibid.,* p. 169.

FIG. 4.1   HUSBAND–WIFE ROLE RECIPROCITY: HUSBAND AS PROVIDER;
WIFE IN STATUS OF COMPLEMENT OR OF JUNIOR PARTNER

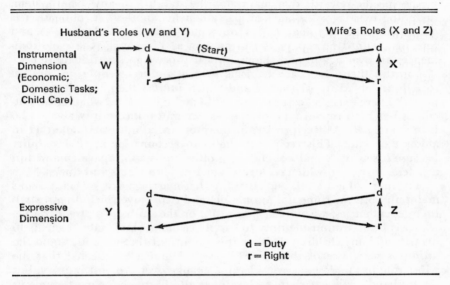

SOURCE: Adapted from Scanzoni, 1970, p. 20. Used by permission.

Husbands and wives each have certain duties to perform for their spouses, and each has certain rights they expect to have fulfilled by them.

Second, the idea held by many that value consensus leads to role conformity (each spouse doing what is expected by the other) which then leads to marital satisfaction and stability leaves unanswered the question, "Why the motivation to conform?" *Why* do some husbands and wives "conform" to each other's expectations? Why do some not conform? Why do some conform more or less than others? Conformity between husbands and wives persists because reciprocity is able to "mobilize egoistic motivations and channel them into the maintenance of the social system . . . egoism can motivate one party to satisfy the expectations of the other, since by doing so he induces the latter to reciprocate and to satisfy his own. . . ." [7] In short, if a husband wants certain rewards from his wife then he must provide the rewards that she wants (conform to her reward expectations); the same is true for her.

Third, we hasten to add that the motivation to reciprocate stems not solely for the exchange of specific benefits, but also from what Gouldner

7. *Ibid.*, p. 173.

claims is an universal norm—i.e., the *moral obligation* to give benefits to those from whom one has received them. It is this moral norm as well as the specific rewards that maintains the stability of any social system, including marriage: "When one party benefits another, an obligation is generated. The recipient (Y) is now indebted to the donor (X) and remains so until he repays." [8] But as soon as Y repays X the cycle commences all over again, and the reciprocal process goes on indefinitely.

Fourth, there are "mechanisms which induce people to *remain* socially indebted to each other and which *inhibit* their complete repayment." There exists a "certain amount of ambiguity as to whether indebtedness has been repaid and, over time, generates uncertainty about who is in whose debt." [9] Reciprocity, furthermore, need not be equal either in amount or kind. This reciprocity helps to account for marital stability because it sets up a chain of enduring obligations and repayments within a system of roles in which *each* role contains both rights and duties.

Turning to Figure 4.1, and recalling that marriage exists when persons maintain both instrumental (economic) and expressive (including sexual) interdependencies, we start at point W_d, or the husband's provider role, which is built around the duty to supply economic and status benefits to his wife and any children. It is terribly important that we understand the *unique* significance of this role. Figures 2.1 and 2.2 indicated that the wife's role has undergone considerable change over the past century, but the husband's role has changed hardly at all. Throughout most segments of modern society, he remains defined as the unique family provider in the sense that if he is healthy, he is *required* and obligated to work. On him falls the responsibility to supply the family's economic well-being in a tangible sense, as well as to supply the less tangible social standing of each family member. [10]

Thus we trace the arrow from W_d to X_r because it is still defined by most Americans as the wife's right to receive the benefits of her husband's provider duties. But the next arrow from X_r to X_d reflects the obligation under which the wife is then placed as a result of receiving those rewards from her husband. She then is obligated (and motivated) to be largely responsible for household duties in the traditional fashion, including care of the children, cooking, cleaning, and so on. The arrow from X_d to W_r reflects the fulfillment of this obligation and corresponds to the husband's *right* to receive these benefits from her. The arrow from W_r to W_d reflects his obligation to keep on performing economically, and so long as these reciprocal processes of exchange continue on

8. *Ibid.*
9. *Ibid.*
10. *See* Scanzoni, 1970.

both sides, they contribute to the maintenance and stability of the husband-wife association.

In her prime role as the "expressive hub" of the conjugal family, she is expected to support and nurture her husband, not only sexually, but in many other kinds of supportive behaviors discussed below. The arrow from X_r to Z_d indicates that as she is rewarded at the economic status level she, in "rectitude and gratitude," is motivated to fulfill this expressive duty, Z_d, which corresponds to the husband's rights, Y_r, to receive it. This, in turn, motivates him to fulfill his expressive duties (Y_d) to his wife, which corresponds to her right (Z_r) to receive these behaviors and further reinforces her own expressive responses to him via the arrow from Z_r to Z_d. The arrow from Y_r to W_d suggests that as husbands perceive expressive rewards being received, they are motivated to continue performing their occupational behavior, similar to the W_r to W_d arrow. And thus the microstructure of marriage is maintained as a stable, ongoing social system, so long as each partner feels rewarded enough by his partner (and obligated enough to him) to maintain the consensus or "negotiated order," that Sprey referred to.

Ultimately, therefore, this chain of processes rests on the degree to which the husband performs his economic role obligations. In simplified form, we may suggest that the husband in modern society exchanges his status for marital solidarity.[11] If we accept as given that expressive satisfactions (companionship, physical affection, empathy) are the obvious goals of modern marriage, and that the major latent goal is status and economic well-being, then we may say that the latent goal influences the attainment of the manifest goal. Specifically, the greater the degree of the husband's integration into the opportunity system (the more his education, the higher his job status, the greater his income), the more fully and extensively is the interlocking network of marital rights and duties performed in reciprocal fashion. The economic rewards he provides motivate the wife to respond positively to him, and her response to him in turn gives rise to a continuing cycle of rectitude and gratitude.

This explanation is one way to account for two relationships discussed in chapter one—first, between social status and satisfaction with the expressive components of marriage. There are several studies which show, for example, that as husband's occupation, education, and income increase, so does the satisfaction of husbands and wives with the three major components of marital expressiveness: *companionship* (someone to do things with—picnics, movies, dancing, etc.—during leisure time);

11. *Ibid.*

empathy (someone to talk to, to share with, someone who understands problems and feelings); *physical love and affection* (someone to love— including sex but not excluding other forms of physical demonstrations of affection).[12]

Second, it also helps to account for the observed relationship be-tween social status and marital stability in modern societies. For the assumption is that greater status benefits generate greater expressive satisfactions, which in turn makes it less likely that satisfied married persons will be motivated to terminate these ongoing exchange processes.

We have only briefly sketched all the implications of Figure 4.1. The interested reader is referred to the original source from which it was drawn for a fuller discussion.[13]

Marital stability, as explained above, is an ongoing process, not a stagnant state. Thus at any point in time a "negotiated order" suggests that a consensus happens to exist. But one or the other partner may wish to *renegotiate* that order. This means that we must make quite explicit something that was touched on only lightly in chapter three.

Bargaining Within Marriage

"Bargaining," says Turner, "may seem like a cruel word to apply to the deliberations of members in the intimate family relationship. But bargaining is simply a general term for any interaction in which the concessions that one member makes to another are expected to be re-ciprocated in some manner, so that over the long run the sacrifices of each will balance out." [14] The bargaining need not be conscious, nor rationally or explicitly calculated. Indeed, it may be quite unconscious, and often husbands and wives may not in the least be aware that they are engaged in bargaining, or in efforts to make the exchange processes between them more equitable:

> Empirical research on bargaining . . . suggests bargaining is normally tempered by a concern with equity. In several studies the subjects have been unwilling to exploit advantageous bargaining positions to the full.[15]

Turner suggests, however, that the concern for generosity and equity may itself be a bargaining point, for the next time round the person who was generous before may, in turn, now expect the other to act in similar fashion. Bargaining, therefore, as an intrinsic aspect of social exchange, is inevitably and inherently part of the reciprocities that hus-bands and wives carry on relative to the instrumental and expressive re-wards that each supplies to the other.

12. *Ibid.;* Blood and Wolfe; Renne; Scanzoni, 1971.
13. Scanzoni, 1970.
14. Turner, 1970, p. 106; *see also* Lederer and Jackson, 1968.
15. Turner, p. 107.

At the same time, it is crucial to distinguish bargaining as part of the everyday processes of exchange and reciprocity from bargaining that is part of the processes of conflict. For in most marriages, most of the time, reciprocity is probably more frequent than conflict.[16] An appropriate analogy might be the relations between management and labor. Most of the time, their interaction is based on an exchange of previously agreed-on rewards, not on conflict over the rewards. From time to time, labor-management conflict (struggle) does emerge, but efforts are made to resolve it, to move once again into "normal" processes of ongoing reciprocity.

In marriage, husbands and wives continually seek rewards from each other, and continually bargain and negotiate over them. But most of the time we may assume that the bargaining eventuates in what Turner calls "willing agreement, to which each is committed because of the benefits he gains from agreement," benefits defined in terms of exchanges.[17] By what means, then, do processes of social exchange evolve into processes of conflict? The line between mere exchange and conflict is an extremely fine one, and actually, reciprocity and conflict are on the same continuum. To distinguish when we have moved from exchange into conflict, or back again into exchange, we need to introduce the phenomenon of power.

Social Exchange and Power

"A person on whom others are dependent for vital benefits has power to enforce his demands. He may make demands on them that they consider fair and just in relation to the benefits they receive for submitting to his power." [18] Figure 4.1 indicates that marital structure in modern society, up to this point in time, is one in which husbands and wives are indeed dependent on one another for vital expressive and socioeconomic benefits. Therefore, husbands and wives do in fact have a certain amount of power (defined as "the ability of persons . . . to impose their will on others")[19] over each other. In the day-to-day processes of social exchange, they bargain with each other in terms of the relative power they possess, and they arrive at certain decisions.

A useful measure of power in terms of some common day-to-day decisions that confront most families has been devised by Blood and Wolfe. Respondents are asked, "Who usually makes the *final* decision about: (1) what car to get; (2) whether or not to buy some life insurance; (3) what house or apartment to take; (4) what job [the husband] should take; (5) whether or not [the wife] should go to work or quit work; (6) how

16. *Ibid.*, p. 109.
17. *Ibid.*, p. 106.
18. Blau, p. 22.
19. *Ibid.*, p. 117.

much money your family can afford to spend per week on food; (7) what doctor to have when someone is sick; (8) where to go on a vacation."[20] The respondent then answers each question in one of the following ways: husband always; husband more than wife; *h* and *w* exactly the same; *w* more than *h; w* always.

Responses to these eight items are then combined into a single index labeled as a measure of "family decision-making." The index has been used repeatedly in the United States and in Western Europe the results have been quite consistent: husbands have more power than wives in decision-making; and the higher the job status of the husband, the more power he has compared to his wife, at least in these eight areas.[21] That is, middle-class husbands tend to decide these kinds of things more often than do working-class husbands, who in turn decide them more often than do lower-class husbands. Thus, middle-class wives have less power in these areas than do working-class wives, who in turn have less power than do lower-class wives.

There are other techniques to measure husband-wife power besides asking who makes the final decision in arbitrarily selected areas. A most glaring deficiency in this approach is that it simply is not feasible for a researcher to think of and list all the potential conflict situations that could conceivably emerge between husbands and wives.[22]

Conflict can erupt at any time and may be related to items which outsiders might consider insignificant or meaningless. For some time, for instance, it has been noted that "tremendous trifles" can emerge in husband-wife interaction and yet be the cause of considerable and serious conflict.[23]

Therefore, another way to assess marital conflict is to ask the respondent to list "the four things that you and your [spouse] have disagreed about most often." In this way the respondent is forced to reflect on the several areas in his-her marriage which most frequently are contested or challenged. No prior assumptions are made as to what areas of conflict might emerge in any given marriage, nor what areas might be bargained over without conflict. Moreover, the fact that these are areas of *frequent* challenge indicates that one or both parties consider them of some importance.

Immediately following the listing of these four disagreements, the respondent is asked "when you disagree about —————— (the first thing cited) who usually gets his way, you or your [spouse]," and so on, separately, for each of the three remaining conflict areas. By this means

20. Blood and Wolfe, p. 282.
21. *See* Lupri, 1969.
22. *See* Scanzoni, 1970, chapter 6, for a thorough critique.
23. *Ibid.*

we get a better idea of which spouse, in an *actual* area of marital conflict, resolves the issue in his favor, i.e., who has more power.

Nonetheless, as might be predicted, when using this procedure husbands and wives again concur that husbands have more power than wives when it comes to conflict-resolution. For example, in regard to the first-named disagreement, 45 percent of those in one sample reported that husbands resolved the conflict in their favor, while only 30 percent reported that wives resolved it in theirs.[24] Some 15 percent volunteered that they "compromised" rather than one spouse or the other simply "having his way." The remaining 9 percent reported they never disagreed about any matter whatsoever. For the second-named item, husbands "got their way" in 35 percent of the households, wives in 26 percent of them. For the third item, husbands, 35 percent; wives, 20 percent. For the fourth item, husbands, 20 percent; wives, 13 percent.

Given the discussion of earlier chapters, it should come as no surprise that husbands are more powerful than wives in routine family decision-making as well as in conflict-resolution, and that higher-status husbands generally have the greatest amount of family authority. Power rests on resources. Husbands, because of their unique relationship to the opportunity structure, tend to have more resources (material, status), hence, more power than wives. And the husbands who have most access to the sources of prestige and tangible rewards—those in the middle-class—have more power than working-class husbands. "Exchange processes," as Blau puts it, "give rise to differentiation of power." [25]

The kinds of exchanges that most husbands and wives carry on are a specific instance of the general domination of women by men. Because husbands have greater access to the opportunity structure than do women, they are in a better bargaining position than wives. So long as husbands keep the provider role to themselves—as uniquely their possession—there will continue to be differentiation of power within the conjugal family, and wives will continue to possess lesser amounts of that power.

Furthermore, several studies have indicated that while working increases the wife's power to some extent, even the working wife has less power than her husband.[26] In most cases, the working wife becomes merely a *junior partner* to her husband. This is because, currently, the basic and underlying dynamics of Figure 4.1 do not change in most families where the wife works. The husband remains the unique provider—the woman remains ultimately dependent on him for material

---

24. *Ibid.*
25. Blau, p. 22.
26. *See* Scanzoni, 1970, chapter 6, for a review of this literature.

benefits and for social status. Up to this time, most working women have not possessed the same degree of commitment to their work as do men, neither has individualistic occupational achievement been central to their work behavior. There is almost unanimous agreement with Degler's observation that the chief concern of most women has heretofore been with "jobs" rather than with "careers." [27]

These jobs are usually defined merely as ways to supplement the family income. For example, in 1967, when husband's annual income was $4,000 to $4,999, 56 percent of their wives worked. Fifty percent worked when husband's income was $7,000 to $7,999; only 39 percent when it was $10,000 to $14,999; 31 percent when it was $15,000 to $24,999; and only 25 percent when husband's income was over $25,000.[28] Thus, the "objective needs" of the family, in terms of what the husband as provider is able to earn, appear to strongly determine whether the wife seeks a job or not.

Even more significant for the attainment of power than the fact of employment is the income which the working wife is able to obtain. Partly because of discrimination against women, partly owing to less than full-time employment, and partly because of their minimal commitment to the occupational world, most working wives earn much less than their husbands. In 1967, for instance, among American husbands earning between $5,000 and $6,000, their working wives earned less than half of what they did. Among husbands whose income was from $8,000 to $10,000, working wives earned only 31 percent of what husbands did. Working wives earned 23 percent of what husbands did if the latter earned $10,000 to $15,000; 16 percent if husbands earned $15,000 to $25,000; and only 10 percent if husbands earned over $25,000.[29]

Thus, if resources brought into the marriage largely shape the relative power that each spouse possesses for bargaining and exchange, then these income data clearly indicate why even most working wives possess less power than do most husbands. Though they have more to bargain with than most unemployed wives, they still up to now have considerably fewer resources than do most husbands.

CONFLICT AND STABILITY–INSTABILITY

THE EMERGENCE OF CONFLICT

Having introduced the notion of power, we are now ready to observe how conflict (defined as "struggle over values, power, resources, in which

27. Degler, 1964.
28. *Current Population Reports*, P–60, No. 64.
29. *Ibid.*

each opponent seeks to achieve his goals usually at the expense of the other")[30] emerges out of husband-wife exchanges. The key seems to be "the fair exercise of power." [31] If a husband or wife makes "demands that appear excessive" to the spouse, he may arouse "feelings of exploitation for having to render more compliance than the rewards received justify. Social norms define the expectations of subordinates and their evaluations of the superior's demands." [32]

Blau goes on to make a point which we shall merely allude to now but shall discuss more fully in the next chapter. It also has to do with the idea discussed in chapter two regarding the consciousness developed by some women in the nineteenth century that they were in fact an oppressed minority group. "There are fundamental differences between the dynamics of power in a collective situation and the power of one individual over another. The weakness of the isolated subordinated limits the significance of his . . . disapproval of the superior." [33] Yet if a number of subordinates protest the unfair exercise of power, this "has far-reaching implications for developments in the social structure." [34] To the extent that large numbers of women might come to define their current situation as an unjust one, to that extent fundamental and far-reaching changes in marital structure would come about, as we shall see later.

When it comes to particular families, wives and husbands are likely to engage in conflict when, in the course of ongoing reciprocities, they perceive they are being "exploited by unfair demands," i.e., they feel they are *unjustly* being asked to bargain away more than they are receiving. They then enter into a situation of opposition in which the critical issue becomes, *how is the conflict to be resolved?* The state of consensus has been disturbed and challenged—can a "new order" be renegotiated, and if so, how? One way to resolve the conflict might be for both partners to compromise and thus to *change* the specifics of the bargaining situation surrounding that particular issue to make it more equitable to both spouses. Another might be for one or the other spouse simply to exert his or her power and resolve it in the way that best suits him—perhaps, but perhaps not, making some concessions to his spouse. Or another way might be for one partner simply to leave that conjugal situation entirely (i.e., separation or divorce).

But before we look specifically at the issue of conflict resolution we need to note three things about the nature of conflict itself that will aid

30. *See* chapter two, fn. 7, p. 31.
31. Blau, p. 22.
32. *Ibid.*, p. 22; also, Turner, pp. 137ff.
33. Blau, p. 22.
34. *Ibid.*, p. 23.

us immeasurably in understanding conflict resolution once we finally delve into it. First, we need to see the distinction between basic and nonbasic conflict. Second, we need to be clearly aware of the positive aspects of conflict; and third, we need to see the distinction between situational and personality-based conflict.

Basic and Nonbasic Conflict

Some persons believe that marital conflict is bad or "dysfunctional," and hence ought to be avoided if possible. Instead, our position has been that given the reward-seeking that is carried on, conflict is inevitable and unavoidable in marriage as it is in any social system. Moreover conflict should not be considered only in its "disruptive" aspects—its potential to tear apart social relationships. Conflict does not *inevitably* threaten social bonds—whether marital or any other.

In this regard, it is critical to recall that *social* conflict refers to struggle over situational elements in which one party sometimes gains to a *certain* degree and the other person sometimes loses to a *certain* degree. Turner, on the other hand, refers to conflict more on the *psychological* level when he claims that "conflict . . . includes the aim of hurting the other person. Conflict is based on an opposition to identities, such that whatever enhances the identity of one combatant damages the other's, and damaging alter's identity becomes a way in which ego can enhance his own identity." [35] Nevertheless, social conflict between persons does not mean that identities must inevitably be hurt. Sometimes, to attack identities may indeed become a strategy of conflict, but social conflict as a larger, more general phenomenon subsumes far more than mere ego attack.

Recalling the analogy from game theory, in a mixed-motive game, it is always to the advantage of each player to see that the other receives rewards too, and that he does not become excessively deprived. We would therefore suggest that marital conflict is generally of a mixed-motive variety, in which the aim of each partner is to gain more of (or maintain) what he thinks he deserves, or is fair, in terms of values, behaviors, resources, and power. Sometimes ego attacks are involved, many times not. Sometimes additional equally severe strategies are employed, including psychological punishment, varieties of coercion, and outright violence.

It was Simmel's contention that conflict is an intrinsic element of social structure; and furthermore that it actually promotes group solidarity and stability. But, queries Coser, "if conflict unites, what tears apart?" [36] In the minds of many people, especially when it comes to mar-

35. Turner, p. 162.
36. Coser, 1956, p. 73.

riage, conflict is generally thought to be divisive, not cohesive. To deal with this question, Coser borrows an idea from political theory that extends as far back as Aristotle. The idea is based on the "distinction between conflicts which concern the very basis of a relationship and those which concern less central issues. Conflicts arising within the same consensual framework are likely to have a very different impact upon the relationship than those which put the basic consensus in question." [37]

By way of illustration, every competitive sport has rules of the game that spell out the specific objectives of the sport. These rules also describe the broad and general outlines of the techniques permissible for players to try to win the game. In football, for instance, it is essential to the "ongoingness" of the game that players on both sides understand and observe rules regarding blocking, tackling, passing, and running. It is this basic consensus agreement that then allows attempts at variations (plays) in passing and so on (i.e., orderly conflict) designed to outsmart the opponent and win the game. But if there were no prior agreement on the rules, there could be no game as we know it. It would become a free-for-all and the spree itself would soon end absurdly if someone decided, say, to hide the one available football. Thus the conflict of ball players against each other *within the rules* actually binds them together and promotes the interests of each team. But lack of consensus over the fundamental rules would make patterned conflict virtually impossible and would thus be likely to dissolve any previously existing relationships between the teams.

We may say, therefore, that there are at least two major types of conflict insofar as their impact on the stability or maintenance of a social group is concerned. The first is negative or "dysfunctional" conflict, i.e., conflict which could terminate the association. This type is more likely to occur when basic values and goals are challenged.

It follows that within marriage, therefore, there may be conflicts which challenge basic consensus, or the rules of the game; and those of a second type which do not—which, instead, challenge less central concerns. It is sometimes difficult to sort out basic from nonbasic issues, but if we refer back to our definition of marriage, we recall the two *basic* interdependencies: the economic and expressive. We would expect, therefore, that whenever basic conflicts occur in marriage, they are very likely to have some connection with one or both of these interdependencies.

There is substantial evidence, for example, supporting the idea that up to this point most Americans (white and black) expect that if he is healthy, the husband is *obligated* to fulfill the provider role.[38] Suppose,

37. *Ibid.*
38. *See* Scanzoni, 1971, for a review of this literature.

however, that a husband unilaterally decides "to drop out of the rat-race," to quit his job and cease entirely to work or to function in his role as provider. The wife will very likely consider this behavior *unfair* and conflict is thereby ignited. Since it is not likely that the wife can physically coerce her husband to return to work, and if she herself does not wish to work, then the only lever of "power" left to her is to threaten to leave him. If this does not alter his behavior, it is then very likely that their marriage could end in divorce.

To take another example of conflict over the very bonds which form the fundamental basis of the relationship, let us assume that one partner comes to believe that sex relations are unnecessary, sinful, or simply too much bother. The other spouse would almost certainly consider that behavior unjust and inequitable, and thus conflict would be ignited in that setting too. And if the spouse cannot muster enough power to bargain (by force or otherwise) the partner into sex relations, then here too dissolution is a strong probability.

What are examples of conflict that are nonbasic, that do not strike at the *core* of marital structure? With regard to the husband's occupation, for example, the wife may want him to change jobs, to get one that will supply a better living standard for the family, whereas he wants to stay in his present job. She may consider it unfair of him to do so, while he may deem it unjust for her to push him in this fashion. Conflict erupts and both partners utilize whatever power they possess to try to achieve their goals. But since the husband is working, the conflict is over something comparatively less central (though very important)—the *kind* of job to work at. We might therefore assume that conflict of this sort is less likely to lead to total dissociation than where he refuses to work.

By the same token, one spouse may consider unjust his spouse's definition of the proper frequency of coitus (too frequent, or not frequent enough), or of the propriety of certain techniques of sexual gratification. These are serious kinds of conflicts, but since they are presumably less basic than the desire and willingness per se to engage in sexual activity, they may therefore be considered relatively less central to the bonds of marital consensus.

This is not to say that if the basic "rules" of marriage are challenged, then dissolution is the *only* strong outcome. Challenge by one partner to a fundamental pattern could also result in basic structural *change* of the relationship, while at the same time it holds together.

Conflict as Positive

More explicitly, it may be said that conflict (basic or nonbasic) that results in change may have a positive effect on the maintenance of a social system such as marriage. This comes about because conflict brings into the open the issue that one or the other partner considers unjust or inequitable.[39] If it is brought into the open, bargained over, and resolved so that the result is satisfactory to both partners, their relationship reverts back to one based on ongoing reciprocities, and therefore solidarity and stability.

If, on the other hand, the partner who felt an injustice should decide simply to repress the matter and not make it a conflict, one result at the *psychological* level could be negative displacement onto other areas. For example, referring back to the spouse who perceives a certain unfairness in his partner's sexual behaviors, if this is not made a conflict issue, then the spouse might unconsciously begin to aggravate his partner in nonsexual areas. He (she) perhaps might ignore her (him) at the dinner table, refuse to go out with her (him), nag in an unreasonable fashion, give undue attention to members of the opposite sex, and in general became a disagreeable person.

At the *sociological* level, failure to engage in open conflict when injustice is perceived may actually result in a less beneficial, less rewarding situation for both persons involved and actually increase the chances for dissolution. Conflict may remove the perceived injustice and thus promote the chances for stability. Blau remarks:

> Opposition is a regenerative force that introjects new vitality into a social structure and becomes the basis of social reorganization. It serves as a catalyst or starting mechanism for . . . change. . . . Opposition activates conflict by giving overt social expression to latent disagreements and hostilities, but it also helps to remove the sources of these conflicts. It is a disturbing and divisive force that ultimately contributes to . . . stability and cohesion. For major cleavages . . . are most likely to occur precisely when recurrent oppositions have been suppressed and conflicts have smoldered.[40]

Marital conflicts, in other words, may enhance stability because they may lead to *change;* and change, by removing the sources of conflict, may make the situation rewarding enough for the partners to want to remain in it. Change within, and of, the association, therefore, is closely linked to its permanence. For example, let us assume that a wife in her early forties, all children grown, wishes to go to work. She merely wants to assume the status of junior partner, as we have described it, not equal partner, as we shall later define it. But her husband insists she must not do it, and he refuses to "allow" her to work.[41] Consequently, she could

---

39. Coser, 1956, pp. 39ff. He draws deeply on Simmel for these ideas.
40. Blau, pp. 301 and 304.
41. *See* Holter, p. 50, for the point that wives who work still seem to seek their husbands' "permission."

simply leave him and dissolve their relationship, or she could repress the idea of employment with the kinds of psychological consequences described above, or else she could conflict with him over the issue and bargain with him into allowing her to work. This latter change in their association could provide a wide range of benefits to the marriage which formerly were not present, and which the husband did not foresee when he initially objected. One result of the conflict and the change may be, therefore, a more cohesive marriage than had existed prior to her working. "Free remonstrance," said Ross, "is a safety valve, letting off steam which, if confined, might blow up the boiler." [42]

Divorce itself, as a type of change, is a way out of a particular marriage, and is a safety valve that has in part contributed to the preservation of the conjugal pattern. Likewise, conflicts and changes that have occurred (chapter two) and that currently take place within virtually all marriages continue to contribute to its preservation as the widely accepted social pattern that we observed in chapter three. Furthermore, there is no reason to suspect that the conjugal (husband-wife) system cannot encompass continued changes toward the equal-partner pattern.

Some persons who prophesy the imminent decease of monogamous marriage do not seem to take account of its adaptibility to allow for conflict, even over the basic rules, and thus to change. Hence to contend that the conjugal family is obsolete or is destroying itself is to be unaware of its ongoing historic evolution—but more of that in chapter five.

Personality vs. Situational Conflict

Finally, we must note the distinction between "realistic" and "nonrealistic" conflict, because it has particular application to marital interaction. Realistic conflict is based on "specific demands within the relationship and [on] estimates of gains of the participants, and . . . are means toward a specific result." [43] In this setting there is a genuinely perceived inequity in the minds of one of the marriage partners. Conflict arises and is followed by efforts to *change* or maintain some part of the distribution of rights and privileges in their relationship. Realistic conflict is the sort we have had in mind implicitly so far throughout the book. It is conflict emerging from and directed toward the structure of *situations,* e.g., should the wife work or not; how to spend the weekly paycheck; and so forth.

What Coser calls "nonrealistic" conflict is based not on situational inequities but, instead, on personality. Some psychologists might balk at the term "nonrealistic" to describe conflict of this type. Therefore it

42. E. A. Ross, cited in Blau, p. 304.
43. Coser, 1956, p. 49.

might be better to talk about the person's *"need* for conflict" as does Coser when he refers to the "need for tension release" and "fulfillment of the tensional need" to indicate what he has in mind.[44] Nonrealistic conflict is not due primarily to structural situations that are deemed inequitable, but rather to the *need* of the person (husband or wife) to express certain inner feelings. This kind of *conflict* may consist of aggressive behavior—once again not directed toward change of a specific situation—but simply to release pent-up tensions and fulfill deep-seated needs. Within the family this may take the form of striking and slapping and perhaps other forms of physical coercion or violence. Because of particular personality characteristics, certain persons periodically engage in hostilities, antagonisms, and conflicts that are clearly not directed towards specific situations or desired changes in role relationships.

Owing to continued physical proximity within marriage, there is obviously a great possibility that nonrealistic conflicts will be vented. Husbands and wives may often "fight" with each other and engage in other kinds of aggressive behavior not because it is goal-directed, or because it stems from some specific situational deprivation, but simply because of a *personality need* to relieve certain tensions that exist at the intrapersonal level. They may do this, of course, and still engage in realistic conflict. Indeed, they may engage in these two kinds of conflicts at different times or simultaneously.

Probably every social scientist will agree that personality variables play an important part in family interaction and stability. The fact is, however, as Winch concluded: "very little has been found in the way of personality traits that are consistent predictors of marital felicity or stability." [45] The distinction between types of conflicts that arise from situational frustrations as contrasted to those based on personality needs may be fruitful for future research. In chapter three, for example, we saw that married persons who have been divorced twice or more are more likely to become divorced again than are married persons who have never been divorced, or divorced only once. It may be, therefore, that there are certain personality variables at work among some persons, resulting, for them, in repeated marital dissolution. Could one of these factors be a sort of "need for conflict"?

Nevertheless, cognizance of this personality dimension in no way undermines the significance of *realistic* conflict in understanding marital dynamics. As Coser indicates, some social scientists (and marriage counselors and therapists) "show no recognition of realistic (situational) conflict or of its functions." [46] There is a tendency instead, on the part of

44. *Ibid.,* pp. 49 and 51.
45. Winch, 1963, p. 712.
46. Coser, 1956, p. 52.

some persons, to treat all conflict as "nonrealistic," i.e., emerging from "personality difficulties." "If the locus of marital conflict lies in the personality," the therapist reasons, "then one must apply therapy to change the personality." If personality is "changed" and people learn how to adjust," and "communicate," then most marital conflicts can be solved, or so some therapists seem to be saying. The focus of attention and analysis becomes the "maladjusted personality" rather than the situation.[47]

If indeed one considers conflict and hostility to emanate from personalities which have a built-in need to be hostile, apart from realistic grievances, then there might be some grounds for the conflict-as-pathology approach referred to earlier. It may be that "unhealthy personalities" do produce "unnecessary troubles." But two things must be kept in mind. First, many who view family conflict as generally negative may be transferring their thinking about personalities to social systems, and such an approach is inappropriate and misleading. Second, those who focus on personality rather than situation as the locus of most conflict often avoid facing the hard realities and difficulties of situational or structural change.

This can be seen in the attitude that for a long time white society took toward the lower-class black family. It was felt that the high rates of desertion, separation, and divorce that characterized these families were due to "weaknesses" among blacks traceable to their cultural heritage as slaves. This was a euphemistic way on the part of some to indicate that black husbands and wives had never learned how to get along with each other, that at the personality level they possessed built-in hostilities which often led to unproductive and sometimes violent conflict and made stability in marriage extremely difficult for them to attain. Therefore, reasoned some, the "solution" was essentially a *therapeutic* one, i.e., "resocialize" blacks, change their values, attitudes, and behaviors.[48]

Recent years have seen this view challenged and the focus put, instead, on the generationally transmitted economic deprivations of poor families, whether black or white. From this perspective, the numerous, basic conflicts which occur in less advantaged homes are not primarily the result of personality difficulties but are traceable, instead, to the economic impingements in which they are caught. The solution, therefore, lies not in individual therapy but in restructuring their economic situation, through such means as family assistance plans that guarantee every family a minimum income.

An even more current example of the contrast between the therapy

---

47. Turner, pp. 154ff.
48. *See* Billingsley, 1968, for a critique of this position.

vs. situational-change approaches pertains to the female sex role. There are some psychiatrists and counsellors who analyze the current demands by females for changes in their rights and privileges from a personality perspective. Some (though not all) maintain that there is a distinct feminine psyche which is ideally suited for nurturant, supportive behaviors, and not for competitive occupational endeavor. Therefore, they say, women who are discontent within this framework and seek for something else need counseling to help them "adjust" to an awareness of their "unique station" in life. The emphasis is on the woman getting help to "overcome her neuroses" and to adjust to the strains of being a modern woman in a rapidly changing society. The suspicion is that if she presses for more female rights she may be just a tiny bit neurotic.[49]

If she feels hostile toward her husband because he is not willing to change the structure of their relationship to allow for more of her rights, or if she engages in conflict with him to bring such change about, some therapists believe this bad because it threatens the stability of their marriage. From the situational perspective, the fact that females seek greater rights is accepted as a social reality and is not explainable at the personality level. Neither can personality explanations account for the inevitability of an overall increase in the frequency of marital conflicts as a result of more and more women seeking these changes.

LEGITIMATE POWER, REWARDS, AND THE RESOLUTION OF CONFLICT

We are now prepared to consider in depth the question of conflict management once it erupts. We have seen that in marriage (as in any social structure) it is inevitable that injustices, inequities, and unfairness will emerge and give rise to conflict. But more specifically, what can we say about the chain of events *between* perceived inequities, conflict, *and* whatever follows—whether it be change or no change, whether stability or instability?

INJUSTICE AND ERUPTION

Let us start at the beginning of the chain and inquire why in some marriages certain behaviors are defined as unjust, yet in other marriages identical behaviors may not be so defined. Compare, for instance, three marriages where the ages of wife and the numbers and ages of children are the same. Mr. Smith refuses to allow Mrs. Smith to work, and Mrs. Smith does not consider this unfair nor does she conflict with him over

---

49. *See* Figes, p. 151; Freud, in Roszak and Roszak, pp. 19–29.

it. But Mrs. Jones considers Mr. Jones's refusal to allow her to work as unfair and conflicts sharply with him over it. And although Mrs. Doe also considers her husband's refusal to allow her to work as unjust, she does not choose to conflict with him over it.

Earlier in the chapter we talked about marital power and its basis in resources provided by one spouse to the other. In addition, sociologists make an important distinction between power that is *legitimate* (called "authority") and power that is not legitimate.[50] Authority is "the direction or control of the behavior of others for the promotion of collective goals, based on some ascertainable form of their knowledgeable consent. Authority thus implies informed, voluntary compliance. . . ."[51] Nonlegitimate power means "control or influence over the actions of others to promote one's goals without their consent, against their 'will,' or without their knowledge or understanding. . . . The emphasis . . . is on the lack of . . . 'consent,' . . ."[52]

Thus, authority implies willing commitment and its extreme form is perhaps expressed in the cliché "your every wish is my command."[53] The extreme form of nonlegitimate power is physical coercion in which a person is literally forced to perform a certain behavior upon pain of death. In between these polar extremes runs the continuum of varying degrees of legitimate power. Power tends to be defined as legitimate (or "right and proper") to the degree that rewards are provided for compliance.[54] Hence, toward the legitimacy or authority end of the continuum, it is the provision of *resources* that is the key element in compliance and approval. Toward the opposite end, it is *punishments* that tend to bring about compliance and conformity, but not approval, for while "compliance can be enforced with sufficient power . . . approval cannot be forced regardless of how great the power."[55]

Blau notes that there are prevailing "social norms" that tend to set the limits within which persons come to believe they are being rewarded fairly, and therefore how legitimate the power is that is being exercised over them.[56] Historically, within marriage, men have been the beneficiaries of what has been termed the "patriarchal ideology," which was simply a set of *prevailing norms* defining how right and proper it was and is for the husband to be the head of the family. Thus as Figure 2.2*A* suggests, a woman in the status of property might have received precious

---

50. Blau, p. 200. *See also* Scanzoni, 1970, chapter 6.
51. Buckley, p. 186.
52. *Ibid.*
53. *Ibid.*
54. Blau, 1964.
55. *Ibid.,* p. 201.
56. *Ibid.,* p. 200 and p. 22.

few benefits from her husband, yet consider his power over her as *legitimate authority* simply because that is what the prevailing sentiments or norms of the time dictated.

Gradually, as the efforts of the Feminists permeated society and family structure and wives gained the status of complement and junior partner, the prevailing norms changed regarding fair levels of rewards to wives in exchange for the levels of compliance or deference that wives show to husbands. However much husbands may have used coercion, or provided only minimal rewards ten to fifteen decades ago, and still maintained legitimate authority over their wives, the situation is very different today. Few, if any, wives today would consider physical force as legitimate, and even more significant—husbands today must bargain for legitimate power based on the levels of rewards they are able to supply their wives.

As we saw in Figure 4.1, the levels of economic and expressive benefits that husbands are able to supply to wives rests largely on their education, job position, and income. We would expect therefore that the higher the husband's socioeconomic position (measured, say, by his job status), the more legitimate authority he possesses. Among families where job status is lower, husbands can be expected to have less authority. Using the Blood and Wolfe eight item index which purports to measure routine family decision-making, it has been found in the United States and elsewhere that as husband's job position rises, so does his power.[57]

However, this index glosses over the difference between legitimate and nonlegitimate power. For example, some studies that have used other measures of family power (such as the one that asks "who gets his way over the thing you disagree about most often"), have found that lower-status husbands actually tend "to get their way" more often than husbands with higher job status.[58] That is, when a conflict issue arises between husbands and wives that is genuinely salient and important to husbands, blue-collar husbands appear to be more likely than white-collar husbands to simply impose their own will and resolve it in the way they think best. For example, conflict may arise over the discipline of an adolescent son for difficulties he gets into at school. The white-collar husband is more likely either to defer to his wife's judgment in the matter or else to work with her at a compromise resolution. The blue-collar husband, on the other side, is more likely to discipline the son in the way he sees fit, irrespective of his wife's wishes or judgments.[59]

The contradiction between those studies which indicate that white-collar husbands have more power, and others which suggest that blue-

57. *See above,* this chapter.
58. Komarovsky, 1962; Scanzoni, 1970.
59. McKinley, 1964.

collar husbands have more, may be solved if we make that all-important distinction between power that is legitimate and power that is not. In one study, the following two-item index was used to assess beliefs in the legitimacy of male authority.[60]

1. The wife should have equal authority with the husband in making decisions.
2. The husband should be the head of the house.

Both husbands and wives were asked whether they strongly agreed, agreed, disagreed, or strongly disagreed with each of the items. It was found that the higher the family income the more likely wives were to agree with these ideas; whereas the lower the income the less likely wives were to agree. In other words, the more income supplied by husbands, the more likely wives were to think in terms of the *legitimacy* of traditional male authority—that the husband should be the family head, and that total equality in family decisions may not always be "practical" or "efficient." The converse is true for wives whose husbands supply less income. As far as wives are concerned, it would seem that husbands with greater income are more able to bargain for the *legitimacy* of their family authority than are husbands with lesser income.

On the other side, among husbands, there were no meaningful differences found by income levels in their beliefs about legitimacy of husband power. Regardless of the level of income (or resources) supplied to wives, they tended to answer both items in more traditional terms than did wives. Thus, husbands appear to believe they ought to have family power on traditional terms, apart from their ability to bargain successfully for it.

The critical point is, then, that the higher the social status of the husband, the more *legitimate authority* he possesses; whereas the lower his status, the more *nonlegitimate power* he seizes.

> A person on whom others are dependent for vital benefits has the power to enforce his demands. He may make demands on them that they consider fair and just in relation to the benefits they receive for submitting to his power. On the other hand, he may lack such restraint and make demands that appear excessive to them, arousing feelings of exploitation for having to render more compliance than the rewards received justify.[61]

And what might influence persons (husbands, in this case) to lose restraint and excessively exploit wives?

> The greater the resources of a person on which his power rests, the easier it is for him to refrain from exploiting subordinates by making excessive

60. Scanzoni, 1970, chapter 6.
61. Blau, p. 22.

demands, and consequently the better are the chances that subordinates will approve of the fairness of his rule rather than disapprove of its unfairness.[62]

Evidently, higher-status husbands feel more secure in their resources and have less need for excessive demands, coercion, or exploitation of wives, yet all the while sensing that their wives ascribe legitimate authority to them. They are more willing to work out compromises with their wives that the latter perceive as fair and nonexploitative. Conversely, lower-status husbands, precisely because they feel less secure in their resources and sense that their wives ascribe less authority to them, are less restrained, more excessive in their demands, and less willing to work out compromises. Instead, they often tend to act unilaterally in a fashion that is perceived by wives as unfair, excessive, and exploitative.

Economic Alienation

But besides income, another set of very important items was used in that same study to distinguish the degree to which husbands and wives accept the legitimacy of husband power.[63] These belong under the general heading of "economic alienation," and reflect the *subjective feelings* about rewards (and deprivations) that husbands proffer to their wives. If we look again at Figure 4.1, for instance, it is critical to keep in mind that the economic rewards being exchanged are not merely *objective* in nature, i.e., amounts of dollars. In addition, there is the *subjective right* of the wife to be rewarded with as low a sense of economic alienation as possible. Economic alienation refers to the sense of gulf, distance, or separation from both the means and ends (benefits) of the opportunity structure of modern society.[64] A low sense of economic alienation means that one feels he is relatively integrated with or participating in the opportunity structure.

To illustrate, one specific dimension of economic alienation is feelings of *satisfaction with husband's job rewards*—rewards such as security, prestige, and "money for the things our family needs." As was the case with family income, it was found that the more satisfied wives were with their husband's job rewards, the more strongly they believed in the legitimacy of their husband's authority.[65] And regardless of how satisfied *husbands themselves* were with their own job rewards, it made no difference in their beliefs about male power. Husbands at all levels of job satisfaction felt extremely reluctant to concede away any traditional male prerogatives whatsoever.

62. *Ibid.*
63. Scanzoni, 1970, chapter 6.
64. *Ibid.*, chapter 2, *passim*.
65. *Ibid.*, chapter 6.

Thinking back to the Smith, Jones, and Doe marriages, let us say that each of the three husbands earns $9,000 per year, and that Mrs. Jones is strongly dissatisfied with her husband's income because, in her view, it falls far short of meeting what she considers to be her family's needs. Because she is so strongly dissatisfied, she also feels very strongly about working in order to attain the family life style she desires. But note the dual injustices she perceives: her husband's job does not supply her with the kinds of rewards that make possible the life style that she considers right and fair; and in the ensuing conflict he refuses to allow her to work —he gets his way, he exercises power even though she considers this exercise of power to be nonlegitimate.

The conflict was ignited in the first place because of what Mrs. Jones deemed unfair rewards, and resolved by what she also deemed an unfair means—her husband's unilateral exercise of what she considers nonlegitimate power. "Exploitation and oppression are punishing experiences, which arouse anger, disapproval, and antagonism against those held responsible for them." [66] It is not the conflict itself that is "punishing" to Mrs. Jones or to any other marriage. *What is more or less punishing is the mode of its management or resolution.* This distinction is often lost on those who say that conflict is "bad" or "unhealthy" for marriage. Mrs. Jones allowed the initial feelings of injustice to erupt into conflict or struggle. Yet in spite of her husband's limited rewards, he exercised nonlegitimate power over her which only served to increase her feelings of injustice because "subjugation . . . can hardly be experienced as just, for it offers no compensating advantages for submission." [67]

In comparison, Mrs. Smith may feel less economically alienated than Mrs. Jones (though their husbands' incomes are the same) and, therefore, not consider the rewards flowing from her husband's income as unjust. Hence, we may say that the perception of injustice depends on the reward levels that the husband supplies to the wife, or the wife to the husband. If they are defined as tolerable, as in the case of Mrs. Smith, then feelings of injustice are less likely to develop. Moreover, because Mrs. Smith defined the rewards as she did, she did not generate a conflict with him over her working; neither, therefore, did she run the risk of a punishment by her husband's resolving the conflict through nonlegitimate power. Hence, reward levels affect not only the definitions of injustice, they strongly affect whether conflict will or will not emerge, and how it will be managed.

The case of Mrs. Doe lies somewhere between Mrs. Jones and Mrs.

66. Blau, p. 229.
67. *Ibid.*, p. 228.

Smith. The socioeconomic reward levels she receives from Mr. Doe are not sufficient to keep her from perceiving that they are unjust, and she also considers inequitable his avowed intention to keep her from working. However, she may define the resources he provides her as at least great enough to keep the feelings of injustice from erupting into genuine conflict.

The notion of economic alienation is obviously quite important in explaining why our three hypothetical wives might perceive similar levels of objective rewards in dissimilar fashion. What might influence feelings of alienation is suggested in Blau's discussion of *reference groups*.[68] The person uses these groups for comparison and evaluation of his own rewards. For instance, Mrs. Smith belongs to a circle of friends who work and who thus enjoy a substantially higher standard of living than would otherwise be possible. Conversely, none of Mrs. Jones's friends work, and these divergent reference groups may in part account for their different feelings of economic alienation.

Another way to think of economic alienation is by the term "relative deprivation" (see chapter one).[69] Reference groups influence persons into thinking how *deprived* they are *relative* to others. Therefore, compared to her friends, Mrs. Smith felt relatively deprived, or not as well off as they. But compared to her friends, Mrs. Jones did not feel relatively deprived. Durkheim was probably the first sociologist to observe that there is no *absolute* ceiling on aspirations for these kinds of rewards in a modern society oriented toward money, power, and prestige.[70]

Consequently, Parke and Glick may be correct when they suggest that divorce rates may decline in the years ahead as more and more people become ever more affluent, from the perspective of the positive consequences of *absolute* economic resources.[71] On the other hand, there may develop a proliferation of reference groups that will question the equity even of increasing absolute benefits. For example, because more and more women are going to work, it may become even more difficult for the Mrs. Joneses to find reference groups that will not create feelings of relative deprivation. A major thrust of Neofeminism, or Women's Liberation, is precisely that—to create feelings of relative deprivation among traditional women.[72] Women in the movement obviously want other women to feel deprived vis-à-vis men, but they also want them to feel deprived compared to women who are fulfilling more "modern" behaviors.

68. *Ibid.*, p. 158.
69. *Ibid.*, p. 159.
70. *See* Mizruchi, 1964.
71. Parke and Glick, 1967.
72. *See* Morgan; Roszak and Roszak.

CONFLICT MANAGEMENT

We are now prepared to delve into the specifics of the resolution of marital conflict. So far we have seen that feelings of injustice, as well as their eruption into actual conflict, are influenced by rewards that are exchanged between marital partners. Likewise the legitimacy of the husband's power depends on the rewards he supplies not only objectively, but subjectively as well.

The above represent general principles that subsume a vast range of husband-wife interactions that could potentially erupt into conflict. To illustrate these principles, we have focused mostly on the sex roles of husbands and wives. That is, we drew (and will draw) on studies that deal with the occupational performance of the husband and on the domestic and occupational behaviors of the wife. We have not meant to exclude anything that might generate husband-wife conflict, and the reader may apply these general principles to as many additional matters as might interest him.

There are, however, several reasons for illustrating and explaining husband-wife conflict by focusing on aspects of sex roles. First, since the basic theme of this study is conflict between males and females, particularly in terms of their sex roles, this discussion is intrinsically linked to the larger whole. Second, the preceding chapters should lead us to the conclusion that of all the matters that might arise in marital interaction, these conflicts are most significant for the development of social theory and public policy. Other matters, including expressiveness, are often linked closely to sex-role definitions. Third, as we saw, long-range trends in divorce rates and in changes in marital structure *up to this time* can be traced to these struggles. And, finally, we shall see that *future* changes in family forms are inextricably linked to these kinds of conflicts as well.

Spiegel has suggested some ideas about marital conflict resolution which he acknowledges to be "arbitrary and incomplete," but at least provide a start in "systematically noting processes in the family which are subtle and difficult to observe." [73] On the basis of his research, Spiegel outlines eleven categories of conflict management. The first five types fall under the general head of what he calls *role induction,* which simply means that one partner changes, while the other does not: "One or the other parties to the conflict agrees, submits, goes along with, becomes convinced, or is persuaded in some way." [74]

73. Spiegel, p. 402.
74. *Ibid.,* p. 402.

Role Induction: Coercion

The first type of resolution under this general head is *coercion*. ". . . it ranges from overt attack to threats of attack in the future, and from verbal commands to physical force. It varies in intensity from mildly aversive manipulations to cruel and unusual torture." [75] Coercion is the apex of nonlegitimate power. In the absence of any rewards that can be used to bargain for a given end, behavior is enforced for which no rewards at all are supplied. Coercion is an extraordinarily punishing way to resolve conflict, but Spiegel notes that "it exists in every family we have studied, and it is probably . . . present in every enduring social system. . . ." [76]

Let us illustrate these several categories by means of Mr. and Mrs. French. This hypothetical couple was married fifteen years ago—immediately upon her graduation from high school and shortly after he spent some years in the army. He too is a high school graduate, and has completed two years of technical training, which enable him to be a lab technician for a large manufacturing firm. He has what most sociologists would agree is a lower-middle-class job. They have two children and Mrs. French has been, most of these years, a traditional housewife or *complement*, as described by Figure. 4.1.

Some seven or eight years ago, Mr. French, after considerable agonizing, made a decision not to attend college, so both he and she are aware that doors to further occupational achievement in his present position are virtually closed to him. Aside from wage increases that his white-collar union periodically negotiates, neither spouse can expect him to make significant gains in prestige, in job satisfaction in terms of "creative expression," in job authority, or in income.

Over the last few years, Mrs. French has developed a sense of economic alienation because of what she considers a limited family life style, and has occasionally worked at low-status jobs simply to earn additional money for the family. Because she occupied the junior-partner status only spasmodically, her husband rarely made that a conflict issue. But in recent months Mrs. French has come in contact with Feminist arguments—through the media and personal contacts—pertaining to individualistic achievement and fulfillment. As a result she wants to attend a local college, obtain a degree, and enter a profession. What motivates her is not *primarily* a desire for money, but a desire for the sense of achievement, fulfillment, service to people, creative expression, prestige,

75. *Ibid.*, p. 403.
76. *Ibid.*

honor, individualistic identity, and self-worth that her chosen field can supply. These are precisely the kinds of rewards that many higher-status jobs in a modern society can offer to persons, though in the past these jobs and their rewards have been restricted largely to white males.

Mr. French, however, opposes her plans for numerous reasons, chiefly because he believes that the necessary changes in his own behavior would be unfair and unjust, not only with respect to child-care and household duties, but especially in the potential threat he perceives to his own occupational role. He could no longer be as "flexible" in working over-time, or in participating in plant activities such as the bowling and soft-ball teams. Most important, his status as *unique* provider with its at-tendant privileges and power would be in serious danger; for it is pre-cisely this status that his wife also wishes to share *equally* with her hus-band, and it would no longer be uniquely his. She wishes to pursue a career with all of its privileges and responsibilities in the same sense that he does. What is more, when she finishes college she will have ob-tained an upper-middle-class job status—her income, prestige, and power will be greater than his.

To Mr. French, this turn of events is perceived as terribly inequitable, and *basic* conflict is generated—conflict over the very "rules of the re-lationship," the core patterns that have bound them together for fifteen years. To resolve this critical kind of conflict, Mr. French *coerces* his wife into staying home, i.e., he issues a *verbal command* that she may not go to school. Nevertheless, as Spiegel notes, the "specific neutralizing technique for coercing is *defying.*" [77] Mrs. French, punished by coercion, simply defies her husband and enrolls in college anyway. Not legally able (she is no longer "property") to restrain her physically (chaining her to the bed), and unable to supply the kinds of rewards that would enable him to exercise legitimate authority to "bargain" her out of her decision, he now finds himself countercoerced, hence, counterpunished. She has seized nonlegitimate power and in effect dares him to retaliate.

Role Induction: Coaxing

Spiegel's second type of conflict resolution—is what he calls *coaxing*. This includes "asking, promising, pleading, begging, and tempting. . . . Coaxing . . . epitomizes desire." [78] Coaxing is a strategy whereby a per-son attempts to bring alter (his or her partner) to his position apart from much genuine bargaining or exchange. The emphasis is on the strategy of forcing alter to capitulate, but short of coercion. Actor begs and pleads and cajoles for alter to come around. The well-known "turning on of tears" is a classic example of coaxing. "If I beg, plead, cry, and pout

77. *Ibid.*
78. *Ibid.*, p. 403.

enough to show you that I really *desire* this, and *simply* because I desire it, you should give it to me; I might thus get you to give in."

After Mrs. French seized nonlegitimate power and enrolled in college, Mr. French retaliated with additional countercoercion by refusing to pay for her tuition and books. This, of course, can also be construed as *basic* conflict since it is an instance of the husband refusing to fulfill a prime rule of the game—support of his wife. Mrs. French then seeks to coax her husband through begging, pleading, and crying to stop coercing her, to allow her to go to school, and to pay the expenses. Mr. French cannot stand the coaxing and so gives in to both these requests.

Nevertheless, as Spiegel suggests, neither coercion nor coaxing genuinely *resolve* conflict—they submerge and defer it only to emerge at a later date. In the French family, shortly after the wife has been in classes for several weeks, Mr. French becomes acutely aware of the added household burdens that fall on him because of his wife's new responsibilities. Since the conflict was not really managed because of her coaxing, it indeed emerges once again. This time *he* tries to coax *her* into dropping out of school. She refuses and he coerces her—he *orders* her to drop out. She continues to refuse, and once again basic conflict occurs between them. He cannot physically restrain her, and he lacks legitimate power to bargain her into another set of behaviors.

On her side, it is quite important to note that her situation is very different from that of a working wife. The latter, at least, has some resources with which to bargain for power—her salary or wages. She can point out to her husband that in spite of inconvenience and burden to him, her income can enhance the family's vacation, or provide better housing, or a new car. Mrs. French has no such resources on which to base power. Her power in continuing in school is just as nonlegitimate to her husband as his is to her in attempting to get her to drop out.

Role Induction: Evaluating

Spiegel describes the third conflict-resolution strategy as *evaluating,* which "in the usual case . . . follows upon coercing and coaxing." [79] Actor responds to alter's behavior by labeling it as "good" or "bad." This includes "praising, blaming, shaming, approving, and disapproving. For example, if alter tries to resolve the . . . conflict through coercion, [actor] may *evaluate* his behavior by saying, . . . 'quit trying to act like a little Hitler!' " [80] In the case of the French family, the wife might indeed respond to her husband's coercion by labeling him a tyrant. He might respond, in turn, by labeling her a "selfish wife," or an "irresponsi-

---

79. *Ibid.,* p. 404.
80. *Ibid.*

ble mother." These labels, as applied to most wives and mothers in American society, would seem to be especially painful conflict ploys, given the socialization of most girls into roles where devotion to husband and children is taught as her supreme duty (see chapter three).

This evaluating and labeling of identities—"tyrant," "irresponsible," —is, according to Turner, a particularly harmful conflict technique.[81] Spiegel notes, however, that if such labeling is accepted, actor might change his behavior. Mr. French might feel "I'm not really a tyrant. I will therefore allow my wife to stay in school." Or Mrs. French may feel that it is repugnant to be considered a "bad mother" and so return full-time to her domestic duties. On the other hand, negative identities can be openly denied: "I am not a tyrant," "I am not an irresponsible mother." In fact, these two denials were used by both Mr. and Mrs. French, respectively. As a result, the labels that Mr. and Mrs. French have "inflicted" on each other introduced considerable bitterness and hostility into their interaction without contributing to genuine resolution of the conflict. Later we shall have more to say about marital hostility per se. The point here is that the negative evaluations and labelings occur simultaneously with attempts at coercion and coaxing.

Role Induction: Masking

The fourth strategy Spiegel describes as *masking:* "the withholding of correct information or the substitution of incorrect information. . . . It includes such behavior as pretending, evading, censoring, distorting, lying, hoaxing, deceiving, and so on." [82] In the case of the Frenches, the wife has been masking or concealing a basic lack of respect for her husband ever since his fateful decision not to attend college. She feels that the decision "stifled his growth and development as a person," and thereby impaired her own self-actualization, since he is not the stimulus to her at this level that she wishes he were. Her decision to attend college only decreases her respect further, since she is willing to seek greater personal development but he is not.

Hence, not only does she feel deprived by her husband in terms of material and status rewards, she feels deprived at this more intangible level as well. A critical point within the conflict process is what happens when *unmasking* occurs. "The role-partners confront each other with what has been concealed or disguised. Where the masking has averted a major [confrontation], unmasking can be extremely explosive." [83]

One day, in the course of their coercions and countercoercions, Mrs. French does unmask and reveal her attitude toward her husband: "I

81. *See* p. 72, this chapter.
82. Spiegel, p. 405.
83. *Ibid.,* pp. 406–7.

don't respect you as a person as much as I did some years ago, and my respect for you decreases with time." So added to coercion, coaxing, and hostile evaluations is the strategy of unmasking. Conceivably, unmasking could result in a change in Mr. French's behavior. He could feel so chagrined at his wife's attitude that he returns to college to regain her respect. Likewise, he may cease offering resistance to her college efforts. On the other hand, the revelation is not likely to alter his behavior in such a dramatic fashion but, instead, will only exacerbate the basic conflict between them still further.

Role Induction: Postponement

A fifth and final induction technique to resolve marital conflict Spiegel calls *postponement*. This is not merely a "negative or passive way" to deal with conflict. "It is undertaken with the expectation in both [actor or] alter that 'in the interval he will change his mind.' The process by which the conflict is to be settled is deferred in the hope of change of attitude. . . . Most role-conflicts in the family are not settled at the moment, but are deferred and taken up afresh, time and time again." [84]

The question for the Frenches, as in any marriage, is "Who has the most to gain from postponing?" In this instance, since Mrs. French is already in school, she has the most to gain by protracting the conflict indefinitely over time. Mr. French has nothing to gain from postponement so he *provokes* or incites "the conflict to appear in full force." [85] Consequently, in their marriage, besides the four strategies discussed above, Mrs. French continually strives for *postponement* of a *final* solution: "Let me stay in school for one year and then let's see what we should do." The longer she stays in school, the more she has gained. For her, the conflict has been "resolved" if a truce, or cease-fire, or state of quiescence exists between them.

Mr. French, conversely, constantly seeks to provoke and resuscitate the conflict because the longer she stays in school the more, from his viewpoint, he stands to lose. And because neither partner can muster enough power to bargain the other into a *genuine* resolution of the conflict, the conflict continues. Therefore, melded into the four ongoing conflict processes already described are, on the one hand, attempts to defer or *postpone* its discussion and genuine resolution, countered, on the other, by efforts to *provoke* it.

In passing, we should underscore Spiegel's observation that few marital conflicts are settled immediately but have, instead, a tendency to drag on over time and to be provoked periodically. It is important to remember

84. *Ibid.*, p. 407.
85. *Ibid.*

this because later in the chapter when we talk about husbands and wives actually making decisions to dissolve marriage or not, one question will be how much unsettled conflict exists, and how punishing these conflicts are perceived to be.

Role Modification: Role Reversal

Spiegel claims that the sixth mode of conflict resolution, which he calls "role-reversal," moves us away from *induction,* in which one partner tries to get the other partner to change, to *role-modification,* in which *both* partners experience some changes in attitudes and behaviors. As might be expected, the modification strategies tend to lead to a more genuine settlement of the conflict, as compared to the usually temporary nature of the induction strategies.

Role-reversal is simply another term for role-taking: "[Actor] proposes that alter put himself in [actor's] shoes, trying to see things through his eyes. Or [actor] initiates the reversal, hoping that alter will do the same. [Actor] may say, 'Well, I think I'm beginning to see your point, but. . . .' Or, 'It doesn't make too much sense to me, but I think I see what you mean.' " [86] At this point it is most critical to recall the distinction between basic and nonbasic conflicts.

For example, in the Frenches' marriage, if their conflict were merely over whether she would work at a job or not, i.e., assume the status of junior partner, role-taking might be more likely to lead to an actual settlement. She could perhaps get him to put himself in her shoes: "I want to enjoy some time away from housework, I want to be able to have my own 'spending money' for clothes," and so on. If the increasing numbers of married women who work are any indication, then over the years more and more women have apparently been able to get their husbands to "role-take" and to understand such arguments.

But the conflict between the Frenches is much more fundamental and primary—it has to do with her moving into the status of *equal partner,* something vastly more significant to husbands than merely having a *junior partner* who also periodically slides into the *complement* status. Sometimes therapists and counsellors give the naïve impression that to engage in marital role-taking or unmasking is almost sure to bring about conflict resolution and thus enhance marital satisfaction and stability. But this view overlooks the type of conflict and its particular significance to each partner. [87]

Mrs. French has unmasked and, in addition to revealing the actual

86. *Ibid.*
87. *See* Stryker, 1957.

level of respect she holds for him, has pointed out to him exactly what she has in mind in her pursuit of occupational achievement. If she then asks him to "role-take" her plans and aspirations, this eye-opener could begin to crystallize in his mind a certain willingness to end their association.[88] Before she had asked him to step into her shoes, he may never have fully realized all she had in mind. Now that he does, Mr. French may perceive that divorce is a more salient possibility than before he had ever engaged in role-taking. And if he communicates this perception to Mrs. French, she too may begin to think more seriously than before that perhaps dissolution will indeed ultimately be the only solution left open to them.

On the other hand, in many marriages there are many conflicts that do not challenge the basic rules of the relationship. In these instances, role-taking, or simply seeing alter's position as alter sees it, may indeed be the first step toward actually settling the conflict, and thus it contributes to the continuity of the marriage.

Role Modification: Joking

According to Spiegel, "*joking* is an outgrowth of role-reversal. . . . The role-partners, having . . . exchanged places . . . and thus having obtained some insight into each other's feelings and perceptions, are now able to achieve some distance from . . . the conflict. They are able to laugh at themselves and each other." [89] For certain marital conflicts (even basic ones), the capability to role-take effectively may indeed give rise to humor as the partners perceive elements of ludicrousness and absurdity in their own behavior as seen through the eyes of the other. Moreover, tension is relieved, and "in play, the role-partners try on for size a series of weird or impossible solutions, out of which is gradually fabricated the substance of the possible solution." [90]

Nevertheless, just as role-taking is no guarantee that a solution will be found or that stability will be maintained, neither is the capability to laugh at oneself. Mrs. French may well be able to see the humorous aspects of her position, but still be in deadly earnest about pursuing her plans for self-fulfillment. "If I cannot be my own person and remain married," she may reason, "I will not remain married." Likewise, Mr. French may be able to joke about his viewpoint regarding his wife's schooling and future plans, but nevertheless adamantly insist that she drop out of school. Basic conflicts such as the Frenches' are seldom, if ever, joked away.

88. *See ibid* for the distinction between role-taking and sympathy.
89. Spiegel, p. 408.
90. *Ibid.*

Role Modification: Referral to a Third Party

Spiegel acknowledges that role-taking and joking are sometimes insufficient, and what may then take place is *referral to a third party*.[91] This may be a member of the kin, a friend, a clergyman, or a professional therapist of some sort.

Spiegel's investigations revealed something that Simmel had long ago described and what Mills has also recently observed, namely, the third party tends to form a *coalition* with one of the partners against the other.[92] The difficulty with that situation is that coalitions tend to *impose* one or more of the inductive strategies discussed above. This does not always happen, of course, and sometimes the third party is able to offer a genuine solution, especially if the conflict is nonbasic in nature.

As we saw, wherever the first five strategies are employed, no real resolution occurs, and thus a third party and any subsequent coalition formation would have only slight influence for the ongoing marital conflict. Moreover, in the case of the Frenches and their particular basic conflict, they are more likely than not to encounter third parties who will side with Mr. French. For after all, it is Mrs. French's behavior and aspirations that are the *immediate* precipitators of these conflicts. Relatives, friends, and many therapists (especially males) may be unable to understand or to sympathize with the nature of her aspirations. Or even if they do, they may place such a premium on the desirability of marital stability that they unconsciously exert pressure on her to modify her feminism.

Figes, for example, documents the enormous influence of Freud on feminine psychology, and thereby, on much professional marriage counseling:

> Freud's ideas on feminine psychology all spring from the tenet that woman's role in life is to stay at home, be passive in relation to man, bear and raise children.[93]

What does that say to a woman like Mrs. French who seeks individualistic achievement? According to Freud:

> She was liable to become neurotic, frigid, thoroughly dangerous to her husband, and might try to compete with males in intellectual pursuits.[94]

Both Freud and his disciple Karl Abraham emphasize the woman's learning to *adapt* to the male.[95] They both held that psychoanalysis and other

91. *Ibid.*
92. *Ibid.*, p. 409, where Mills's findings are discussed.
93. Figes, 1970, p. 142.
94. *Ibid.*, p. 144.
95. *Ibid.*, p. 145.

forms of counseling and therapy would aid her in her adaptation. Figes contends that even though today there are numerous schools of therapy, much Freudianism permeates almost all of them.[96] She cites the contemporary psychologist, Helene Deutsch, as one example of therapists who support female adaptation to the male:

> "What is common to all these [feminine] types is facility in identifying with man in a manner that is most conducive to the happiness of both partners. . . . To the woman falls the larger share of the work of adjustment: she leaves the initiative to the man and out of her own need renounces originality." . . . These are the "ideal life companions for men" —"They are the lowliest and most unaggressive of helpmates and they want to remain in that role; they do not insist on their rights—quite the contrary. They are easy to handle—if only one loves them." [97]

Not only therapists, but many persons (more men than women—see chapter five) in Western society probably still retain the notion that the key function of the wife is to "adapt," to "adjust" to her husband—particularly in occupational behaviors—in order to preserve harmony and marital stability. "After all," comments Figes, "if both partners in a marriage consider their own wishes and interests as equally important, conflict is bound to arise." [98] The point is that for basic conflict in general, and for the Frenches' conflict in particular, the utility of a third party is highly problematic. And, if most available third parties would simply form a coalition with Mr. French in order to try to *induce* Mrs. French to *change* and to *adapt* to her husband, the third parties would be of no utility at all, for reasons discussed above.

The same conclusions would apply, of course, if perchance Mrs. French were able to locate a third party who would form a coalition with her. It would then be Mr. French who would be *induced* to change his position completely. Rare indeed, therefore, is the arbiter who can satisfactorily resolve basic conflicts. Almost by definition, each actor's own position is so critical or basic in importance to him that it becomes extraordinarily difficult for him to alter it significantly enough to accommodate the other's position.

Role Modification: Exploration

According to Spiegel, *exploration* is the next strategy of conflict resolution. In exploration the partners "probe and test each other's capacity to establish a novel solution." [99] Third parties may or may not have been

96. *Ibid.,* p. 148.
97. *Ibid.,* p. 149.
98. *Ibid.,* p. 149.
99. *Ibid.,* p. 409.

helpful in setting the stage for these probes. "Actor and alter propose and reject possible solutions." [100] In both words and actions, efforts are made to determine what alter will or will not settle for.

Once the processes of conflict management have moved to this point, questions of legitimate power, resources, and bargaining become extremely salient. In the case of the Frenches, let us assume that both partners are actually interested in serious explorations to see if the basic conflict over her schooling and her long-range plans can be settled. An illustrative probe might be Mr. French's promise that he will cease to provoke conflict over future situations and prospects if, *in exchange,* she promises to attend college only part-time, to which he pledges he will not object at all.

Or she might probe with the possibility that she will bear the full cost of her schooling through loans from her relatives. Moreover, she will arrange to have a relative come in and do most of the housework and cooking and care for the children. Thus she promises to relieve her husband of financial and domestic burdens, if he will stop provoking conflict and simply allow her to remain in school full-time.

And so it goes—each partner making proposals and counterproposals, testing the other, and bargaining to see if each can emerge with a solution that is satisfactory to both partners in this *mixed-motive* conflict. For Mrs. French perceives that it is in *her best interests* that Mr. French consider the ultimate solution as genuinely satisfactory. Mr. French, too, perceives that *his best interests* will be served if his wife is actually satisfied with whatever solution at which they might arrive.

Role Modification: Compromise

Compromise, says Spiegel, may follow "a sufficient amount of exploration," when each partner is willing to *accept* "some change in the goals each desired or in the values by which they were guided." [101] After probing, exploring, and bargaining, the hard question becomes, what will each partner actually accept for the reality of their day-to-day lives? For example, if Mr. French had more resources and legitimate power he might be able to bargain his wife into accepting his proposal of her going to school part-time. But he lacks sufficient power to obtain this kind of solution, and so Mrs. French will not accept it because it will double the number of years she has to go to school; and since she is already in her thirties she does not feel she can lose any more time. Hence, that kind of *compromise,* that potential end to the conflict, is not made a reality.

100. *Ibid.*
101. *Ibid.*, p. 410.

From his perspective, Mr. French rejects her compromise solution because he does not believe that kinfolk ought to interfere unnecessarily in their family's internal affairs, and also because he does not really want her to make rapid progress toward her degree. He perceives that once she has it, their relationship will change even more radically than it has already. Hence, the compromise she offers is not acceptable to him, yet she lacks the legitimate power to bargain her husband into accepting it, and so the conflict continues. Compromise was wanted by each side, and potentially, could have emerged from either side, but it did not, and the conflict is not resolved.

Role Modification: Consolidation

Consolidation, says Spiegel, is the last step in conflict resolution where there has actually been a mutually arrived-at compromise. "Even though [actor] and alter establish a compromise, they must still learn how to make it work. . . . The new [behaviors] still have to be worked through and internalized by [actor] and alter as they discover how to reward each other in playing the new roles." [102] Had, for instance, Mr. French accepted his wife's compromise, the consolidation would have involved learning how to live in the new situation she proposed. Or had she accepted his solution, she would have had to consolidate, i.e., to put into everyday practice, those new modes of behavior by attending college part-time.

In many marriages, compromises over conflicts are followed by periods of consolidation. Then the newly established behaviors become part of the ongoing processes of consensus, of reciprocity and exchange described earlier. Only if and when these newly consolidated behaviors give rise to feelings of injustice and inequity will conflict emerge once again. And if conflict does erupt, then attempts at management will also emerge along the lines we have just described.

REWARD–COST RATIO AND MARITAL STABILITY

We have seen that economic and expressive rewards operating together supply strong motivation to remain in a marriage, and that *punishments* in the form of conflicts "resolved" through nonlegitimate power constitute motivation to exit from a marriage.

One of the most critical issues, therefore, in understanding marital stability, instability, and change is the *ratio* of costs (punishments) to rewards that actor experiences and perceives. One could predict that the

102. *Ibid.*

greater the rewards and the fewer the costs, the more likely that the marriage will continue. For example, a marital partner who perceives ten rewards but only one punishment is more likely to want to remain in his marriage than someone who perceives three rewards and ten punishments.

Considerable investigation is necessary to tell us much more about the linkage of the cost-reward ratio to marital stability. Some divorced persons, for instance, will state that there was little or no conflict in their former marriage—they simply grew tired of or bored with each other. In such instances, while the level of punishment is quite low, so is the reward level. Other divorced persons maintain that while they fought all the time and had bitter conflicts, they really liked each other through it all—their sexual gratifications, as an example, were optimal to the end, and in some cases even thereafter. In those instances, while rewards were apparently satisfactory, punishments were evidently too high to be tolerable. Among most marriages that end in divorce, however, our prediction would probably hold true, i.e., instability occurs when there are few rewards and high costs.

Let us return to the Frenches to determine what each partner perceives his cost-reward ratio to be and what connection this has with whether their marriage changes and persists. Mr. French has a white-collar job in an occupation usually classified as lower-middle-class. As such, he is able to supply Mrs. French a moderate level of objective economic rewards in the form of income. And as we saw above, Mrs. French does not feel more than moderately rewarded by allayed feelings of economic alienation. Subjectively, she wishes she were more satisfied with the level of benefits she is receiving, both in their tangible and non-tangible (prestige, status) aspects.

As indicated above, there are studies which show that the more objective rewards a husband is able to supply to his wife, the more positively both partners evaluate their expressive relations. There are also studies which indicate that the greater the feelings of economic alienation, the *less positively* do partners evaluate marital expressiveness.[103] So in the case of Mrs. French, the moderate levels of objective *and* subjective economic status rewards she receives in her marriage are correlated to similarly moderate levels of expressive or socioemotional rewards.

Mr. French, like most husbands in modern society, does not expect direct economic rewards from marriage in the same sense that wives do. Nevertheless, since the conjugal family is the major unit of consumption in modern society, and since it is through consumption symbols (house, clothing, car) that status, respect, worth, and identity are assigned to him

103. Scanzoni, 1970, 1971.

and his family by others in the community, Mr. French does expect that the kind of life style (consumption symbols) he supplies his family will reflect back on him as a source of reward or benefit. Mr. French, therefore, aware that his job supplies only moderate levels of objective economic rewards, may feel moderately economically alienated in terms of these rewards, and also in terms of the kind of life style they make possible for his family. He feels alienated primarily because his wife has communicated her sense of dissatisfaction and economic alienation to him.

Moreover, for the Frenches, as Figure 4.1 suggests, the moderate level of economic rewards she receives motivates her to respond to her husband only moderately at the expressive level, which in turn motivates him to respond moderately toward her. Therefore, both Frenches seem *moderately* satisfied with their marital rewards. They may feel less rewarded, say, than many upper-middle-class couples, where the evidence indicates *greater* satisfaction with both the economic (objective and subjective) and expressive dimensions. On the other hand, they may feel more rewarded than many working-class couples, where the evidence shows *lesser* satisfaction with both dimensions.

Turning to the cost or punishment side of the ledger, let us look first at the notion of hostility. Conflict, as defined here, involves a struggle to change some aspect of the husband-wife reward and power structure. Hostility is distinct from conflict and can be defined as "feelings of anger, opposition, and antagonism that may often—though not inevitably—eventuate in behavior that could be described as offensive and/or aggressive." [104] Thus hostility, whether latent or manifest, may sometimes, though not always, emerge during some of the processes of conflict management—especially in its first five segments.

The following four items were used in one study to measure husband-wife hostility.[105]

1. How often would you say you have a big blow-up with your (spouse)?

2. How often do you get so angry with your (spouse) that you refuse to talk?

3. How often do you get so angry that you swear at your (spouse)?

4. How often do you get so angry that you tell your (spouse) you don't love (him–her) any more?

104. On the distinction between conflict and hostility, *see* Coser, 1956. *See also* Scanzoni, 1970, p. 136.
105. *Ibid.*, p. 137.

Using a composite index of these four items, it was found that as objective rewards (occupation, education, income) increased, and as economic alienation decreased, both husbands and wives reported less hostility in their marriages.[106] Put another way, as the level of objective rewards drops and levels of alienation increase, marital hostility is likely to increase also. Another study among blacks tended to support this conclusion.[107] For the Frenches, therefore, the frequency of hostilities between them during conflict is likely to be relatively moderate. That is, punishments of the sorts described by the above four items, plus related behaviors such as striking or slapping, are likely to be less frequent, say, than for working-class couples, but more frequent than for upper-middle-class couples.

Finally, there is the question of nonlegitimate power as a punishment or cost. We saw earlier that the lower the status of the husband the less restrained and the more excessive he is in exercising nonlegitimate power. Mr. French, for instance, is more likely to be defined by his wife as exercising nonlegitimate power than is an upper-middle-class husband. In the case of the conflict over her staying in school or not, Mrs. French perceives her husband's attempts to seize nonlegitimate power as a *severe* punishment because she desires very much the rewards (sense of fulfillment, satisfaction, individual achievement) that the opportunity structure offers her.

Consequently, in terms of her own reward-cost ratio, the several rewards just described are moderate, but in one respect, at least, the costs are very high indeed. They could potentially go even higher if he manages to "coerce" her into dropping out of school. For Mr. French, those rewards are also moderate, and certain costs are also high in that his wife is, in fact, exercising power that he considers unfair and nonlegitimate by her staying in school. There are obviously many additional kinds of rewards and costs in the Frenches' marriage, as there would be in any marriage. These have been omitted here for the sake of space and simplicity. But given the kind of reward-cost ratio that each of the Frenches perceive, what is the likelihood of their marriage being dissolved?

There does not seem to be much likelihood of compromise and change in the direction sought by Mrs. French. Such a change would in fact represent a new form of the family and we will discuss it more in the next chapter. Nor is Mrs. French likely to settle for the minor changes proposed by her husband. As to whether or not each partner defines his reward-cost ratio as favorable enough to want to stay in, or unfavorable enough to want out, it should be made quite clear there are no *fixed* or objective criteria of favorableness that *any* outsider can impose on

106. *Ibid.*
107. Scanzoni, 1971, p. 272.

any marriage. Many persons remain in situations that, to outsiders, appear to contain a very unfavorable reward-cost balance; others leave situations that, to outsiders, seem quite favorable indeed.

Thibaut and Kelley's notion of "comparison level for alternatives" (*CL alt*) is useful here, because it is defined as the "point employed in deciding whether or not to remain in the interaction. . . . It can be looked at as the lowest level of reward which the individual will accept in order to continue in the relationship." [108] When that point, *CL alt*, is reached by either or both partners, it represents the breaking point at which the reward-cost ratio is deemed *too unfavorable* to maintain the relationship any longer. When that lower threshold is reached by either or both Frenches, it is then that dissolution (usually repeated separations and reunions, then generally followed by legal divorce) becomes a very strong probability.[109]

Until *CL alt* is reached, theirs, or any marriage, is likely to continue simply because the reward-cost ratio is, at the least, "barely tolerable," and in some cases may even range into the "acceptable," or perhaps on into the "very favorable." In the case of the Frenches, since neither partner wishes to change his goals, and especially if Mrs. French insists on staying in school beyond the first year, it appears that the level of costs (hostilities, coercions, and countercoercions) will range so high for both partners that *CL alt* will be reached and dissolution follow, assuming that rewards remain constant (or perhaps even drop and thus generate still greater hostilities).

CONCLUSION

The prime goal of this chapter has been to explore the dynamics of marital structure from a sociological perspective. We have sought to go beyond notions of "consensus" and "complementarity," as a basis for marriage maintenance, change, and dissolution. Marriage, as any other social system, is an arrangement based on an exchange of rewards and benefits, i.e., on reward-seeking. In most marriages, most of the time, processes of bargaining and reciprocity characterize the ongoing interaction. At certain times, feelings of injustice ignite conflict—some of it fundamental in nature, but most of it less critical or basic. Husbands and wives attempt to manage or resolve the conflict, usually resulting in some changes in the distribution of rights and privileges.

During both the ongoing reciprocities and the conflicts, husbands consistently appear to have more power than wives. When this power is

108. Cited in Scanzoni, *ibid.*, p. 223.
109. *See* Goode, 1956.

used in nonlegitimate fashion, it becomes defined as a punishment. The ratio of rewards to punishments, *as defined subjectively by either spouse,* is a determining factor in deciding whether to remain married or not. When the ratio becomes too unfavorable and drops to the low point of *CL alt,* then dissolution becomes quite likely.

To illustrate these processes we have focused largely on conflicts and changes surrounding sex-role definitions because this approach appears to be most significant both for theoretical and practical understanding of family structure and process. At the same time the ideas presented here are sufficient to begin to explain and understand most areas of husband-wife reciprocities and conflicts. The emphasis on sex-role conflicts within marriage as a microstructure dovetails and is intrinsically a part of male-female conflict at the broader or macro level. In the real world, it is virtually impossible to separate micromarital conflicts from macrolevel male-female conflicts. It seems apparent that each is at the same time the cause and consequence of the other.

V. The Future of Marriage

While prognostication within social science is always hazardous because of the paucity of our theory and measurements, predictions about future marriage forms are exceptionally perilous. Nevertheless prediction is the goal of this chapter, and to attempt it we need to recall points made earlier. First, we said that conjugal marriage as a widely accepted, predominant social pattern seems to be persisting.

We also said that historically, the status of wives has changed. While they possess more power today than they did 170 years ago, most still remain subordinate to their husbands—they possess less power in the processes of bargaining and exchange that characterize marriage in modern society. Finally, underlying the entire discussion so far has been the theme of reward-seeking and conflict. Our argument has been that long-term changes in marital forms in general, as well as changes in the frequency of divorce, are largely the result of female pressures for greater equity of rewards against male resistance to give up their ancient prerogatives. Where do these pressures take us in the future?

ALTERNATIVE APPROACHES TO FAMILY CHANGE

Before we discuss change emanating out of these pressures, we need to consider a variety of ideas about family change, all of which share in common their failure to make change explicitly contingent on the issue of male-female conflict. While it is difficult to sum so vast a literature the following is representative:

> To what extent does the American family structure contribute to the optimum development of the human potential of its members? *This is*

perhaps the key question for the assessment of any alternative structure [italics supplied].[1]

Another spokesman says that marriage should be changed into a "human-actualizing contract." [2] Otto also writes of "The New Marriage: Marriage as a Framework for Developing Personal Potential." [3] Obviously, there is no inherent contradiction between the goals of modern Feminism and the "optimum development of persons" within marriage.[4] Indeed one of the complaints of the Feminists is that present arrangements do not allow many women to develop themselves fully as persons —witness Mrs. French in the preceding chapter.

Many social critics of the family assume that a substantial number of men and women share a deep dissatisfaction with marriage as it is now constituted and wish to change it into a search for a more "growth-producing, person-releasing, self-actualizing experience." The impression conveyed by some critics, however, is that men and women are beginning this quest *together* on a fairly *equal* footing. There is only slight allusion to the current subordination of women by men and to the means by which this subordination will be overcome. Little systematic attention is paid as to just what the connections are between the present exploitation of women and future family forms. It is almost as if the status of women is forgotten and submerged in the new quest for meaningful sex and marital relations.

AMERICAN COMMUNES

Downing, a California psychiatrist who has considerable first-hand experience with "the diffusely evolving subculture I call the 'Society of Awakening' . . . [of which] the type of most current interest and notoriety is the so-called 'Hippie' tribal family," comments that "in the tribal families, while both sexes work, women are generally in a service role, such as waitress, masseuse, and secretary. *Male dominance is held desirable by both sexes. The recognized dress* is in a semirural or western style which *emphasizes sexual differences.* The women tend to wear long dresses and long hair, while the men tend toward the western or frontier clothing of boots, rough-woven clothes, and outdoor jackets" [5] [italics supplied].

Downing claims that "this new family form appeals most strongly to the mobile, youthful, white middle-class, who . . . have experienced

1. Otto, 1970, pp. 4–5.
2. Satir, 1970, p. 57.
3. Otto, 1970, p. 111.
4. See Farson, et al., 1969; Otto, 1970, *passim;* Skolnick and Skolnick, 1971.
5. Downing, 1970, pp. 122–23.

in their own lifetimes the disruption and isolation springing from their parents' depression-generated preoccupation with 'getting ahead,' gaining material satisfactions, security, and the social status of power and conspicuous consumption." [6] Persons in these tribes "have a semipermanent economic, sexual, and dwelling relationship on the basis of common needs and interests . . . : artistic, economic, productive, social-sexual, or ideologic." While in the tribes or communes observed by Downing there is no sexual promiscuity as defined by the larger society, sexual mores are much less rigid and much more open to continuous redefinition.[7]

Of particular interest in this description of an allegedly new family form is the reversion to traditional patterns of male dominance. Members may periodically work outside the tribe but when they do they tend to pursue stereotyped sex-role jobs; and men appear to retain their traditional power in deciding how, when, and where to allocate funds.[8] And since members of the tribes seem to pair off and form somewhat exclusive sexual attachments (though sex outside the pair does occasionally occur just as it does in "straight" society), it would seem that the social status of the woman in these communes is not much different from what it is among marriages in the larger society, i.e., complement or junior partner. There may be more psychological satisfactions owing perhaps to greater spontaneity and less conventionality, but no one can be certain of that until an empirical test is carried out comparing women and men from tribes and the larger society.

Lack of rigorous research is, of course, the major problem in arriving at valid generalizations regarding commune living or other experimental family forms. It might be charged, for instance, that Downing's sample is not representative of communes located elsewhere, where sexual equality is an explicit goal and is attained. Berger and his colleagues were able to carry out a much more rigorously conceived research program than was Downing, and their report is based on some twenty communal tribes in Northern California. These tribes were mostly rural and engaged in subsistence farming, as contrasted with Downing's tribes which were mostly urban-based.

Berger et al. conclude that a subsistence-type commune is not a place

> likely to be praised by serious women's liberationists, since women seem
> to fall naturally into doing most of the traditional "women's work." But
> this is less a matter of traditionalism than of natural functionality and
> available skill. If a woman is in possession of special skills, she will gener-

6. *Ibid.*, pp. 125–26.
7. *Ibid.*
8. *Ibid.*

ally not spend a great deal of time in the kitchen or milking goats. If she isn't, she's likely to cook rather than haul lumber or do other heavy work which men are better equipped for.[9]

Note that it is only the exceptional woman who makes it out of the kitchen—most remain there. A man with no special skills is not relegated to the kitchen. And it is quite likely that, as in the larger society, given men and women of equal skills, men will be given the more challenging and desirable tasks. Moreover, in a section on leadership and authority, Berger et al. make no reference whatsoever to the existence of any explicit ideology supporting sexual equality within the communes they studied. Instead, the information which is reported leaves the distinct impression that leadership and authority remain pretty much in the hands of males, just as in the larger society.[10]

Finally, in a separate report on her observations of a rural commune, Davidson tends to corroborate Downing and Berger et al.:

> With couples, the double standard is an unwritten rule: the men can roam but the women must be faithful. There are many more men than women [an observation that Ellis makes about group marriage in straight society, *see* below] and when a new girl arrives, she is pounced upon, claimed, and made the subject of wide gossip.[11]

The double-standard is close to the epitome of female subjugation and has been one of the prime targets of Feminists for many decades past. Yet in this "new form of the family," it remains very much in evidence.

In reporting on the tasks necessary for subsistence, Davidson expands on Berger et al., and her description sounds remarkably like any anthropological account of primitive marriage:

> It becomes clear why, in a community like this, the sex roles are so well-defined and satisfying. When men actually do heavy physical labor like chopping trees, baling hay, and digging irrigation ditches, it feels very fulfilling for the woman to tend the cabin, grind wheat, put up fruit, and sew or knit. Each depends on the other for basic needs—shelter, warmth, food. . . . There is a direct relationship between work and survival. . . . The most repetitive jobs such as washing dishes or sawing wood [are said by the hippies] to be spiritually rewarding.[12]

In most agrarian groups (whether hip or straight), when existence depends on success in agricultural efforts, men have almost always come to exercise greater authority than women. Because of their greater

---

9. Berger, et al., p. 517.
10. *Ibid.*, pp. 517ff.
11. Davidson, 1971, p. 531.
12. *Ibid.*, pp. 539–40.

physical strength, and because they are unhindered by childbearing and nursing (childbirth seems to be frequent in hip communes, owing to the low value placed on mechanical contraceptives that interfere with spontaneous love, lack of money for physicians who could prescribe the pill, and the high value placed on children[13]), they are free to pursue the most "functionally significant" tasks for the maintainance of the tribe or family. That is, in the maintenance of any social system, certain tasks are defined as more *critical* and requiring more specialized abilities and skills than others. In an agricultural setting, the more physically demanding tasks tend to be defined as the province of men. Land must be cleared, plowed, planted, cultivated before grain can be grown, ground, and baked. Men could perform *either* the less-demanding tasks (grinding and baking) or the more physically strenuous. Women tend to be limited to the less-demanding tasks which are also less critical in a chronological hierarchy of importance—for if there is no grain grown there is no bread. Men can both grow grain and grind it if they have to —women are limited in growing it, owing to physical and childbearing factors. For as recent anthropological evidence shows with regard to primitive tribes worldwide: "although certain tasks are universally masculine, virtually none is always feminine." [14]

Therefore, because men tend to monopolize those tasks which are more functionally significant than those performed by women, this kind of task performance becomes a resource on which to base legitimate power. Men usually have more power than women in an agrarian setting for precisely the same reasons they do in an urban setting—they possess greater access than women to the resources on which to base power.[15] This phenomenon occurs not only in American communes, but also in that most established of all communes, in which experiments to alter family forms have been most effective—the Israeli kibbutzim, which we shall shortly discuss.

But first we need to acknowledge that authority based on functional significance could conceivably be challenged in some communes, whether urban or rural. Women could, on purely ideological grounds, demand equal authority. They could argue that part of the reason for leaving straight society was to get away from the sex-role "hangup." And, in spite of their lack of resources with which to bargain for equal power with their men, they might somehow be able to convince them to share power equally. In the absence, however, of any empirical evidence for this almost utopian situation, equality based on ideology alone seems problematic at best.

13. Berger, et al.; Davidson.
14. Clignet, 1970, p. 355.
15. This point is made quite clearly for most African tribes by Southall, 1961, p. 59.

THE BAMENDA TRIBE

Second, we must take note of a special case that deviates from the fore-going generalizations, which are otherwise quite valid worldwide, a sub-sistence agriculture tribe in West Africa, the Bamendas, where women have a remarkable degree of power. Indeed, when and if the tribe modernizes and its members become more urbanized or involved in industrial pursuits, their women could stand to lose much of the power they currently possess.[16] The base for their power lies in the fact that *the Bamenda women own the crops on which tribal members depend for existence.*[17] To be sure, men own the land, but women are totally responsible for planting, cultivating, and harvesting the crops, with only occasional help from a male to move a firmly emplanted stone. As a result of this control of the means of production, the rights, privileges, and power of women, both legally and informally, are fairly equal to those of men.[18]

Kaberry also notes that "women tackle their jobs with interest, zest, and pride—attitudes which are communicated at a very early age to their young daughters. . . . The responsibility of women for agriculture is not regarded by them as a sign of inferior status. On the contrary, it confers status and is bound up with feminine self-respect and dignity. They take all the pride of an expert in their work. . . ." [19] Pregnant women work in the fields until the eve of delivery, then rest for approxi-mately 20 to 25 days. They then return to the fields, taking the infant with them only for the first month or two, after which it is left with a nursemaid.[20]

Bamenda men engage in and control the trade and sale of small goods and thus make their contribution to their own (conjugal) family's well-being in this fashion.[21] "Marriage is, among other things, a business partnership, the husband having an appreciation of his wife's powers and the expectation that she will contribute to the family exchequer. On her side, her own sentiment of self-respect demands that she does so." [22]

This brief description of the Bamendas suggests certain conclusions. (1) Evidently women can successfully perform the physically demanding tasks of agriculture as well as men.[23] Once land has been cleared, there

16. Kaberry, pp. 153–54.
17. *Ibid.*, p. 35.
18. *Ibid.*, pp. 48 and 103.
19. *Ibid.*, pp. 70–71.
20. *Ibid.*, pp. 80–81.
21. *Ibid.*, p. 140.
22. *Ibid.*, p. 147.
23. Some other societies give evidence of this also. *See*, for example, a discussion of Philippine women in Hunt, 1965. For a further discussion of status and power among African women, *see* Paulme, pp. 1–15; Clignet.

seems to be no inherent reason why women should be relegated to the kitchen as they seem to be in most American communes. (2) Women can come to enjoy their work, be strongly committed to it, and gain from it a major source of identity, self-image, self-respect, and self-worth. Mothering, nurturance, and other traditionally feminine tasks are apparently not the sole intrinsic sources of female identity and fulfillment. Work can take on the same meanings for women as it does for men. Women can occupy the status of family provider in the same sense as does the male. It is not necessary that there be only one *unique* provider. (3) Relative equality of status and power between husbands and wives appears to be quite possible. And when equality exists, it is not so much the result of ideology, or of a quest to reactivate marriage, or to endow it with new meaning. Instead, equality of status and power emerges from access to the resources necessary to bargain for it. In the case of Bamenda women, this means control of vital economic resources.

THE KIBBUTZ

At this point, we turn to what is, up to now, the most significant and long-lasting attempt to change the structure of marriage and the family. This experiment also represents another instance where change has not come *directly* out of a struggle between the sexes for equality of status and power. The first of the kibbutzim was founded in 1909 and was made up of groups of European immigrants to the wilderness areas of Palestine.[24] They were socialists who believed in communal ownership of property and in the inherent spiritual value of agricultural endeavor.[25] "The emancipation of the woman and complete equality of the sexes was one of the most important goals of the kibbutz from its inception."[26] Nevertheless, the specific behaviors requisite to attain this goal were not at all clear to the kibbutz pioneers: "they arose from necessity, became standardized later, and were eventually incorporated into the kibbutz outlook as an essential element of its way of life."[27]

The necessity was that the early kibbutzim could simply not afford to allow each wife the luxury of remaining home to care for her children. Every able body was needed in the fields, and so the idea of a communal nursery gradually evolved. One or two women could thus care for all the children, releasing many more for agricultural production. Presently, in the kibbutz, a married couple "lives in a single room. . . . Their meals are eaten in a communal dining room, and their children are reared in a communal children's dormitory. . . . The education and socialization of

24. Ben–Yosef, p. 14.
25. *Ibid.*
26. Leon, p. 131.
27. Ben–Yosef, p. 63.

kibbutz children are the function of their nurses and teachers, and not of their parents." [28] When a couple wishes to marry, they request a room from the kibbutz. Upon granting of the request, they are married, "their union is *ipso facto* sanctioned by society." [29] However, around the time of the birth of the first child, a legal ceremony occurs in order to grant the child legal rights in accordance with Israeli law:

> . . . Most of the functions of the typical nuclear family have become the functions of the entire kibbutz society. This is so much the case that the kibbutz as a whole can almost satisfy the criteria by which Murdock defines the family. . . . The kibbutz can function without the family, because it functions as if it, itself, were a family; and it can so function because its members perceive each other as kin. . . .[30]

In these respects, therefore, the kibbutzim are similar to American communes, or nonblood-related extended families, as described above by Downing. But there are several critical respects in which they differ substantially. First, we have been able to find no explicit statement of an ideology of sexual equality among reports on American communes. Such an ideology has always been present in the Israeli communes. Second, the kibbutzim have never been geared toward mere subsistence agriculture, or meagre life style, as seems to be the case with many American communes—both rural and urban. The significance of work is downplayed in American communes, with only enough effort expended to make existence possible.[31] Work, on the other hand, remains highly valued in the kibbutzim, not only for its own sake, but also because of the profits that surplus production brings to the group-family as a whole.[32] And even where a particular American commune might seek to develop more than subsistence agriculture, the reported widespread use of hard drugs would seem to make such a goal difficult to attain.

At the same time it must be noted that there are some American communes that do not permit the use of hard drugs at all. They may do this for many reasons, but one that has received widespread publicity in the popular press is religious in nature. The so-called Jesus-freaks, or Jesus-people represent a more extreme and emotional variety of this Christian communal living, but there are other Christian groups which are more subdued in their life style and in their approach to the larger society.[33]

All these Christian groups share a desire to reestablish some of the

---

28. Spiro, 1968, pp. 70–73.
29. *Ibid.*, p. 71. Compare with our discussion of "trial marriage" in chapter three.
30. *Ibid.*, pp. 73–74.
31. Downing, pp. 123–24.
32. Ben–Yosef, pp. 60ff.
33. "Church Commune: A Shared Concern," *Chicago Daily News* (March 22, 1971).

principles of communal living practiced by the Christian church at its inception, principles which have largely disappeared except among certain Catholic orders. The last century saw numerous examples of these American religious communes.[34] Journalistic reports on current groups indicate that a large proportion of the members of these Christian communes were once part of the drug scene, and that these new groups provide a way to reject what they now consider to be its undesirable elements while retaining many of its more attractive features such as sharing the household and joint economic efforts. There is no indication, however, that the status of women has been altered in these kinds of communes, any more than in any of the nonreligious groups.

The third significant way in which American and Israeli communes differ lies in the fact that in the years immediately following their founding, kibbutz women actually participated as fully as men in the agricultural endeavors:

> When the original settlers first settled on the land, there was no sexual division of labor. Women, like men, worked in the fields and drove tractors; men, like women, worked in the kitchen and in the laundry. Men and women, it was assumed, were equal and could perform their jobs equally well.[35]

Therefore, it was possible for individual kibbutz women to have as much functional significance as men. Many women had the resources to bargain (if they wished) for positions of power and leadership. On the other hand, within the American communes studied, there is no evidence of this level of equality of power and leadership, even on a potential or temporary basis.

For a time, kibbutz women appeared to have had the potential resources to achieve genuine sexual equality. Their status was in some respects potentially comparable to that of Bamenda women, with one most significant exception—they did not own the crops exclusive of men. Lacking, therefore, any sure base of woman-power, over time, kibbutz men gradually began to assert authority and to edge women back into traditionally feminine tasks of the kitchen and nursery. Ostensibly, it was argued that many agricultural tasks were too strenuous for women, and that since 1946, the need for military security "demanded" that men be out in the fields in case of ambush or attack.[36] Spiro claims that:

> For obvious biological reasons, women could not undertake many of the physical tasks of which men were capable; tractor driving, harvesting, and other heavy labor proved too difficult for them. . . . A pregnant woman

34. Tyler, pp. 108–195.
35. Spiro, 1956, cited in D'Andrade, p. 179.
36. Ben–Yosef, p. 79.

... could not work too long ... a nursing mother had to work near the Infants House. ... As ... the birth rate increased, more and more women were forced to leave the "productive" branches of the economy and enter its "service" branches. But as they left the "productive" branches ... their places ... were filled by men.[37]

Several investigators concur that there is considerable discontent among kibbutz women.[38] In particular, women appear to be most dissatisfied with their economic activities. Apparently the general levels of dissatisfaction are owing mainly to the gap between their *actual* economic and social status and what their ideology tells them it should be:[39]

With the exception of politics, nothing occupies so much attention in the kibbutz ... as "the problem of the woman. ..." It is no exaggeration to say that if Kiryat Yedidim should ever disintegrate, the "problem of the woman" will be one of the main contributing factors.[40]

In a study of one kibbutz it was found that women make up only 35 percent of the membership of committees that control it, only 25 percent of these committees are chaired by women, and in the top governing body, only 20 percent are women.[41] Other studies report similar levels of powerlessness among kibbutz women.[42] This lack of power is explained by Leon and others in terms of the kinds of economic tasks in which most kibbutz women are engaged. For example, in one kibbutz (representative of most kibbutzim), 5 percent of the women do administrative work, 5 percent are medical nurses, 10 percent are in agriculture, 15 percent in teaching, 25 percent in child care, and 40 percent are in kitchen work, cleaning, and sewing.[43]

Even in the kibbutz, there remains a difference between productive work and that which does not bring in direct income.[44]

The question boils down largely to a question of social status. There is an unmistakable tendency in many cases to look down upon household services in the kibbutz as being unproductive, since they do not produce revenue.[45]

37. Cited by D'Andrade, p. 179.
38. Spiro, *ibid.;* Rabin, 1970, cites numerous studies to this effect.
39. Spiro, 1956; Rabin, 1970; Leon; Ben–Yosef.
40. Spiro, in D'Andrade, p. 178.
41. Leon, p. 134.
42. Cited by Rabin, 1970.
43. Leon, p. 134. *See* Rabin, 1970, for this same point and similar data.
44. *Ibid.,* p. 136.
45. Ben–Yosef, p. 81.

There seems to be a fairly clear-cut division between masculine and feminine occupations in the kibbutz. The former are mainly the economically productive occupations—the ones that create capital. The latter are the ones involving service and consumption. . . . The managerial functions are almost entirely in the hands of men. . . . It is not only physical strength that determines the occupational role; the dominant male segment has acquired the positions of control and power in kibbutz society.[46]

Thus, the chief reason for lack of woman-power and sexual equality in these communes, explicitly dedicated to a classless social order, is essentially the same reason as in American communes—women have considerably less access to the means of production, the economic resources which are ultimately necessary if the group is to survive as a group. It is also, as we saw, the reason why wives in urban marriages have less power and lack equality.

It is precisely for these reasons that many keen Feminist thinkers have criticized socialism as the means to end female inequalities. Mitchell, as one example, argues that the traditional slogan of the socialists, "let us abolish the bourgeois family," "must be rejected as incorrect today." [47] The slogan was an "abstract entity," she claims, and never specifically spelled out as to how the goal should be attained.[48] "The strategic concern for socialists," Mitchell argues, "should be for the equality of the sexes, not the abolition of the family." [49]

In many kibbutzim the conjugal family, as known in modern society, was in large measure abolished, and in its place an extended, nonblood family was established. Yet sexual inequality continues. The countries of Eastern Europe and Russia are socialist, or actually one-party communist countries. As we saw in chapter one, there have been governmental attempts in Russia to impose elements of sexual equality. But both there and in other communist countries, men continue to dominate in and out of the family.[50] In the democratic Scandinavian lands, socialist parties have shaped public policy for a number of years, but still there is not yet anything like genuine sexual equality.[51]

We shall return to cross-national comparisons later, but it is useful to attend for a moment to Mitchell's point: it is more strategic and significant to focus on sexual equality rather than abolishment or change or family experimentation. The consequences of sexual equality, she claims,

46. Rabin, 1970, p. 303.
47. Mitchell, p. 172.
48. *Ibid.*
49. *Ibid.*
50. Field; Geiger; Dodge.
51. Dahlström.

"are no less radical" and more "concrete and positive" than "abolishing the bourgeois family." Skolnick and Skolnick, in contrast, argue that "the functional problem of the family today is the recreation of extended family ties without kinship. . . . The problem is . . . [to recreate] the kind of social solidarity that exists in the extended family. . . ." [52] They see present conjugal patterns as a social problem, as repressive, and unable to allow full self-actualization. The solution, they contend, is a return to the tribe, in one form or another, as described so far in this chapter. To be sure, they wish, at the same time, to retain "equality, individuality, and freedom," for which they say "the conjugal family stands." [53]

But we have found no evidence so far of any ongoing, nonblood-extended family that guarantees genuine equality of freedom and power to women. After all, the traditional blood kin provided much less freedom for the masses of women than does conjugal marriage. Therefore, to talk about the tribe as a "new" family form may disguise a contradiction in terms. What seems to be new is merely intimate ties not based on blood. Sharing of material goods and child care is an ancient feature of the blood kin. From the woman's standpoint, the nonblood tribe certainly is *not* new, if she remains as subordinate as she did in both blood kin and conjugal family forms.[54] If a family form is to be devised which is *genuinely new* and actually *radically different* from the past, it must be one in which the conditions of the larger social structure will allow women to share power and status equally with men *on a permanent basis,* and not merely temporarily, as was the case in the early kibbutzim.

ADDITIONAL VARIATIONS IN SEX, MARRIAGE, AND FAMILY PATTERNS

Before discussing what such a form might be like, we need to consider some additional attempts to experiment with family patterns, none of which, however, make sexual equality a central issue.

The Intimate Network

Stoller, for instance, agrees with those critics who contend that "the isolated family may well be incompatible with a richer investment in family experience." [55] His solution is something short of the nonblood kin described above, though it aims for the wider solidarities espoused by the Skolnicks. It is called an "intimate network of nuclear families," and defined as "a circle of three or four families who meet together regularly and frequently, share in reciprocal fashion any of their intimate

52. Skolnick and Skolnick, pp. 29–30.
53. *Ibid.,* p. 29.
54. Ben–Yosef, p. 84.
55. Stoller, p. 151.

secrets, offer one another a variety of services and do not hesitate to influence one another in terms of values and attitudes. . . . Such an intimate family network would be neither stagnant nor polite but would involve an extension of the boundaries of the intimate family." [56]

Stoller argues that the intimate network preserves the privacy that most American families seem to value, while at the same time it allows for interfamily support and correction that he feels would aid many families in their quest for satisfaction and fulfillment. The key issues of his plan center around how malleable the boundaries of the intimate family will be. In most cases they will include the sharing of problems, recreation, services (babysitting and so on), and funds during crises. [57]

Group Marriage

The intimate network, in which separate households are maintained, sex is not shared, and money is not held in common, must be distinguished from *group marriage* in which "four to fifteen adults are living together, sharing labor, goods, and services, bearing and raising their children in common, and engaging in promiscuous sex relations, so that every male in the group has intercourse, at one time or another, with every female in the group." [58] The wide variety of sexual partners and possible uncertainty as to who exactly the father of a particular child might be distinguish this arrangement from the hip communes described above. In spite of occasional interpartner sex, "exclusive sexual access is a norm that runs deep" among those communes.[59] Likewise, in most cases, the natural father of a commune child is known, and biological parents and children identify with each other.

But in genuine group marriage, these considerations are obviously irrelevant. Ellis reports that most such groups report a high rate of turn-over—persons move about from one group marriage to another—which further complicates accurate knowledge about parenthood.[60] Likewise, says Ellis, group marriages have difficulty in lasting for more than a few years. They "seem to break up for one reason or another, particularly for nonsexual reasons." [61] The Constantines, however, report that the group marriages they studied gave evidence of stability and permanence.[62] They also conclude that group marriage is a "structure limited to a

56. *Ibid.*, p. 152.
57. *Ibid.*
58. Ellis, p. 85.
59. Berger et al., p. 514.
60. Ellis, p. 90.
61. *Ibid.*, p. 89.
62. Constantine and Constantine, 1970, p. 44.

relative few." [63] Ellis concurs, indicating that "it seems very doubtful . . . that a great many people will rush into group marriages in the near future. . . . [It] is a logical alternative . . . for a select few." [64]

Mate-Swapping

Although Ellis argues that the numerous difficulties of establishing a *permanent* household in which group sex and marriage are practiced will probably tend to retard its growth and acceptance, *wife-swapping*, he says, is a simpler variety of group marriage, for all that is involved is *sex*—not sharing a house, children, or money.[65] There are no *reliable* data on the number of people who actually engage in wife-swapping, how frequently they do so, for how many years, or with how many other persons, though it is a subject currently much discussed in the popular press. "Swinging" is the preferred term among mate-swappers because " 'wife-swapping' is objectionable, as it implies sexual inequality, i.e., that wives are the property of husbands." [66] (Later, we shall discuss the link between "free sexual expression" and genuine equality between the sexes.) According to Denfeld and Gordon, swingers "have higher levels of education than the general population; 80 percent of one study attended college, 50 percent were graduates, and 12 percent were still students. They are disproportionately found in professional and white-collar occupations. They tend to be conservative and very straight." [67]

Swingers tend to locate each other through swingers' clubs, swingers' bars, personal reference, personal recruitment, and advertisements in underground papers and swingers' magazines.[68] There seem to be four basic rules of the game of swinging.[69] One is that a particular couple "swings together," that is, one partner does not engage in extramarital sex unless the other is present. Another has to do with paternity. Couples are careful not to swing while they are trying to have a baby (and during pregnancy) so that the father of the child is, in fact, the legal one. Interestingly, swingers try to conceal their behavior from their children by hiding swingers' publications, and sending the children to relatives during swingers' parties.[70]

A third rule pertains to discretion. Swingers are supposed to keep their behavior secret from friends so as not to risk losing respectability. Single

63. *Ibid.*
64. Ellis, pp. 96–97.
65. *Ibid.*, p. 93.
66. Denfeld and Gordon, p. 471.
67. *Ibid.*
68. *Ibid.*, p. 472.
69. *Ibid.*, pp. 473–75.
70. *Ibid.*, p. 474.

persons and blacks tend to be excluded from white swingers' parties. Finally, sexual jealousy is combatted through each partner's pledging no emotional or love involvement with the outside partners—just physical interest, and that their own marriage commands "paramount loyalty."

As Denfeld and Gordon indicate, swinging is not a "new structural form" of marriage but rather an adjunct to traditional marital patterns.[71] It is an "extension of marriage boundaries" that includes sexual sharing but not sharing of the kinds of emotional and pragmatic elements found in the "intimate network," nor sharing of the economic and childrearing functions of the genuine group marriage:

> The swinging suburban party differs, then, from the conventional cocktail party only in that it revolves around the sexual exchange of mates.[72]

Serial Monogamy, Polyandry, Polygyny

We know from chapters one and three that reports of serial (or what Alpenfalls calls "progressive") monogamy are greatly exaggerated.[73] Contentions that a considerable number of people hop about from one legal union to another are simply unsubstantiated by available evidence. Since the number of people married more than twice is only a tiny fraction of the total population, this practice can hardly be considered a trend or a coming alternative to present conjugal patterns.

What about polyandry (one wife, two or more husbands at the same time) and polygyny (one husband, two or more wives at the same time)? There are no data on the extent of such patterns, and we may expect them, like group marriages, to be quite limited in numbers, and temporary insofar as particular arrangements are concerned. Neubeck speculates broadly and suggests that in some *unspecified decade or century in the future* such patterns might emerge because:

> In the new era, it is taken for granted that both men and women want variety in their relationships, a variety . . . yielding more experiences and bringing out different facets of oneself, a variety enabling people to affirm themselves more fully, to actualize themselves more powerfully.[74]

Unfortunately, Neubeck devotes only a few words to the fact that both polyandry and polygyny are quite ancient, that they currently exist in many nonwestern countries, and that polygyny is by far the more common pattern. Of particular interest here, in view of our overall theme of increasing female self-determination worldwide, is Clignet's observation,

71. *Ibid.*
72. *Ibid.*
73. Alpenfalls, 1970.
74. Neubeck, 1970, p. 106.

after careful study of the effects of modernization on several African tribes in which polygyny was common:

> . . . schooling of the female population . . . has had a negative effect on polygyny. . . . Not only have educated women refused to belong to polygynous families, even as senior co-wives, but they have been in a position to force males to change their domestic attitudes and behavior.[75]

Polygyny, as Clignet shows, tends to generate a whole series of family conflicts, many of which are punishing in the sense described in the prior chapter (i.e., nonlegitimate power is used to settle them). The real defect of polygyny, says Paulme, "lies in the absence of conjugal intimacy, in the distrust between the wives themselves, or their jealousy over each other's children. Possible causes of discord are endless. . . ." [76] Whether more than a very few Western women, at any time in the foreseeable future, will adopt a pattern that educated women in other societies are slowly coming to reject seems exceedingly doubtful.

Two-Stage Marriage

We saw in chapter three that we cannot be sure about the actual numbers of people who live together without legal sanctions. Nor can we be certain as to whether more or less people are behaving this way compared to 1870, 1900, or 1945. Nevertheless, we saw that the long-range trend of legal marriage has been upward since 1890. So far anyway, it appears that whatever the frequency of informal trial marriages, the vast majority of persons also eventually want it legally supported.

Margaret Mead and others, however, suggest that two-step (or stage) marriage patterns ought to be formalized or written into law. The first stage she calls the *individual marriage:* "a licensed union in which two individuals would be committed to each other as individuals for as long as they wished to remain together, but not as future parents. As the first step in marriage, it would not include having children." [77] In addition to provision of the most efficient contraceptives available, the couple would also have to be guaranteed swift access to safe and legal abortion in the event of unintended pregnancies. According to Mead, significant economic ties between them would be minimal with no support or alimony if they decide to end the arrangement. Its purpose is chiefly to give "young people a chance to know each other with a kind of intimacy that does not usually enter into a brief love affair." [78] Besides legitimizing their living

75. Clignet, p. 33.
76. Paulme, p. 9.
77. Mead, 1970, p. 80. *See Redbook* (April, 1968), where Mead seems to tone down her original arguments. *See* chapter three, fn. 22.
78. Mead, 1970, p. 81.

together and their sexual access, it would "allow them to part without the burden of misunderstood intentions, bitter recriminations, and self-destructive guilt." [79] This arrangement would represent an extension of the ongoing exchange processes, described in chapter three, prior to what Mead calls the *parental* or *actual* or *permanent* marriage.

Individual marriage is an attempt by its proponents to *rationalize* the present system of mate selection and marriage formation so that couples can live together in an actual legally sanctioned situation. It is hoped, thereby, that couples can develop more accurate perceptions of what kinds of economic and expressive rewards they can hope to obtain from their mate and what their mate expects from them. They can experience processes of bargaining and exchange within an actual marriage, as well as how conflicts are resolved and how often these turn out to be punishing. In short, some sense of a reward-cost ratio can be developed within a framework loose enough to make extrication, if desired, quite simple indeed.

If both persons decide that the ratio is favorable enough, they then apply for permanent status and a license to be parents. Mead suggests that before the couple be so licensed, they undergo considerable screening to determine that they are indeed prepared to take on the serious responsibilities of *parental marriage*. Even so, she allows that after some years persons who have gone through both stages might nonetheless wish to part, and divorce would be arranged, "but much more slowly" than is often the case under present arrangements.[80] Mead also notes that some persons might never wish to leave the *individual marriage* stage, and remain there with the same person for many years, while others within this same stage might want to shift partners more often. She claims her plan would simultaneously "dignify individual relationships for young people," and "recognize parenthood as a special form of marriage." [81]

Nonheterosexual Approaches

These involve arrangements in which persons deliberately choose to live in households apart from members of the opposite sex. They may live alone or with one or more household mates. They may at times engage in heterosexual behavior or they may choose to be celibate. As one representative of Women's Liberation puts it:

> Only when we accept the idea of celibacy completely will we ever be able to liberate ourselves. Until we accept this completely—until I say I control

79. *Ibid.*
80. *Ibid.*, p. 83.
81. *Ibid.*

my own body and I don't need any insolent male with an overbearing manner to come and gratify my needs—they will always have over us the devastating threat of withdrawing their sexual attentions and, worse, the threat of our ceasing to be even sexually attractive.[82]

Some of these persons may carry on homosexual or lesbian relationships with their house mate, others may not. By our earlier definition of marriage, if persons share both economic and expressive (including sexual) interdependencies, then ongoing homosexual and lesbian relationships can be classified as "marriages."

Increasing numbers of states are legalizing one-parent adoption. Men or women may choose to live with natural or adopted children apart from the presence of an adult of the opposite sex. It is, of course, quite common among *lower-class blacks* (less than one-third of the total black population) for women to head households that contain comparatively large numbers of children. The evidence shows, however, (1) that most of these women would prefer to have a husband who is a stable provider; (2) that they wish they had fewer children.[83] These women have virtually no choice about the poverty, marital instability, and family size with which they are forced to contend. The lower-class black matrifocal situation is a necessary technique of survival to cope with white economic discrimination against the black male.[84] It cannot be construed as a purposively chosen "newly emerging family form." Where blacks have the economic resources to let them choose, they gravitate toward the predominant form of marriage.[85]

One of the reasons black mothers in poverty resent their situation so much is that they cannot provide opportunities for their children to enable them eventually to escape poverty and the matrifocal pattern. On the other hand, among better-educated women and men, white and black, where there is a free choice to be a single parent, chances are good that the number of children will be held to one or possibly two and that these children will possess opportunities comparable to other children at the same status level.

Miscellaneous

Into this category would fall all *remaining* discussions of, and actual experiments with, marriage and family forms, however minor or insignificant they might be[86] (all those, that is, who do not make male-female conflict and sex equality explicitly part of the process and outcome).

82. As told to Bernard, 1970, pp. 42–43 in *The Futurist.*
83. Rainwater, 1966.
84. Billingsley, 1968.
85. Scanzoni, 1971.
86. Some general comments are found in Orleans and Wolfson; *see also* Otto, *passim;* Farson et al.; Skolnick and Skolnick.

Moreover, we must keep in mind that these experiments, whatever they be, besides the more major ones just discussed, are limited to a relatively few out of the hundreds of millions of persons in Western society:

> Sociologists, psychologists, and others who have considered non-traditional forms of marriage and family life generally seem to concur with each other . . . that the majority of individuals living in this society, at this time, would most likely choose monogamous living were they given free choice from a variety of alternatives.[87]

We concur with Otto and with most researchers that monogamy will be with us for some time to come. But we also see the possibility of significant structural changes emerging *within* the exceedingly broad parameters of monogamous heterosexuality. These changes continue the long-term processes begun around 1800. They emanate from the steady pressures of some women for genuine equality of status and power in the belief that only in this way can they truly enjoy genuine "self-actualization" in marriage. Indeed, apart from substantial changes in the position of women, attainment of fulfillment-type goals is extremely problematic, as illustrated most vividly in the kibbutz.

RADICAL MOVEMENTS AND THE EQUALITY OF WOMEN

The question must be raised as to what impact radical social movements might have on the status of women both in and out of marriage. In spite of the fact that the kibbutzim, American communes, and the remaining marriage experiments seem to have had very little impact on the status of women, might not their status be altered by such militant groups such as S.D.S., the Black Panthers, and so forth? Brown claims that "the goal of the New Left is to dismantle outworn institutions and replace them with better arrangements." [88] Therefore, alongside protests against other inequities would not equality for women also be a central issue?

Apparently not, at least from the standpoint of some women who have been part of the New Left. Jones, for example, argues that local S.D.S. groups rarely if ever allow women into top policy-making positions.[89] Morgan suggests that men of the Left consider women's suffering "irrelevant or titillating." [90] It seems to be as difficult for radical as it is for moderate men to take seriously the complaints and demands of Feminists.

87. Otto, 1970, p. 187.
88. Brown, p. 225.
89. Jones, pp. 217–18. The S.D.S., however, has passed a "National Resolution on Women," which recognizes women's grievances. See pp. 254–59, in Roszak and Roszak.
90. Morgan, 1969, p. 242; See also Piercy, p. 432.

Women make at least two major complaints against the male Left.[91] One, women are forced into the subordinate positions there as they are in the larger society. The routine clerical work, the legwork, the dirty work—all of this falls to women—while men carry out the decision-making processes, exert power, and bask in prestige. Morgan's second complaint is even more fundamental, for it touches on the relationship between sexuality and sex equality.

For many years, long before the New Left, some "professional observers" of the family had asserted that contraception and a new morality had liberated women.[92] Because they no longer had to fear pregnancy, they could now be on an equal footing with men. The alleged sexual revolution and sexual freedom were equated with equality of sex roles. But Morgan and others make it quite clear that this equation simply does not exist. Men in and out of the Left, whether radical, liberal, or conservative, may be very happy to accommodate women who perceive themselves liberated sexually. Among many of the marriage experiments described earlier in the chapter, for example, observers report that there are more men than women involved.[93] Many men welcome female sexual experimentation and female rejection of former taboos on premarital and extramarital sex. Nevertheless, *sexual freedom is in no way necessarily correlated with sex equality.*

Numerous spokeswomen for Women's Liberation have pointed out that the *Playboy* philosophy, endorsing removal of sexual restraint, does nothing to alter the stereotype of woman as a sexual object to be wined, dined, and enjoyed by the affluent white man who has "made it" in life. Morgan, for instance, claims that "the so-called sexual revolution . . . functioned toward women's freedom as did the Reconstruction toward former slaves—reinstituted oppression by another name."[94] Whether among respectable middle-class swingers, or hip New Left groups, men and women may exchange sexual favors, but women are still subordinate to men in family, economic, and political behaviors. Until women have the resources to bargain with men for equality of power and status within these social structures, sexual experimentation means little. The New Left experience demonstrates that women cannot bargain for power and prestige on the basis of sexuality alone. When women try, men simply *exploit* them in the classic sense of the term—take something (sexual favors) from them, but give nothing substantial (power, status) in return. Men, according to Morgan and others, are only too happy to take part

91. *Ibid.*
92. Figes, pp. 85–86.
93. *See* Ellis, in Otto, 1970.
94. Morgan, 1969, p. 243.

in the sexual revolution as long as it does nothing to fundamentally alter male-female roles, which it has not.

An analogy to the continued subordination of women by current radical and liberal groups is found in the French Revolution. "Women played a very significant role in the French Revolution," first in the intellectual ferment that led up to it.[95] Eighteenth-century Paris contained many salons sponsored by elite women to which intellectuals of both sexes came to debate and plan the destiny of France. Second, these same women played an active role in the genesis of political parties which actually planned and executed the Revolution. It was the deputation of women, for instance, that invaded the Assembly at Versailles and brought the king back to Paris.[96]

But once the Revolution was accomplished, the position of women actually became less than what it was prior to it. "In 1793 the National Convention suppressed all women's clubs and societies, closed the salons, and denied women all political rights." [97] Prior to the Revolution, some women had actually been able to vote and to sit in legislatures—but no more. Figes attributes this renewed subordination to the anti-Feminist influence of Rousseau and comments "that the women of revolutionary France were thoroughly conned. . . ." [98]

Both historically and currently, therefore, it seems clear that male political and social radicalism stops short of radical sex equality. Other forms of inequality are taken seriously by activist men, but not this form. Perhaps one reason is that men have difficulty in defining women as distinct or *independent* from themselves. At all social class levels, in both black and white communities (except for the black lower-class), wives, up to now, have been dependent on husbands for their status in society. Men have been very much concerned that they themselves possess equality with other men. As long as they have this form of equality, they feel that "their *own* women" (wives, daughters) share this equality with them and all the benefits that flow from it. Therefore, as long as men define women as economically dependent on and socially *indistinguishable* from themselves, it is exceedingly difficult for men to perceive the issue of female inequality as a genuinely serious one.

BLACK MEN AND WOMEN'S LIBERATION

And while it is difficult for most white men to take the issue seriously, it appears even more difficult for most black men. For, as one black Feminist acknowledges:

95. Figes, p. 100.
96. *Ibid.*
97. *Ibid.*
98. *Ibid.*

If women were suddenly to achieve equality with men tomorrow, black women would continue to carry the entire array of utterly oppressive handicaps associated with race. Racial oppression of black people in America has done what neither class oppression nor sexual oppression, with all their perniciousness, has ever done: destroyed an entire people and their culture.[99]

What seems of utmost importance to most black men is to develop black self-determination and obtain educational and occupational positions viable enough to enable them to fulfill (if they wish) the model described in Figure 4.1.[100] There is nothing inherently white or bourgeois middle-class about that model. It does describe the husband-wife situation that has emerged in modern society largely as a result of male access to the opportunity structure. Black men, for so long denied access to opportunity, now strongly seek opportunity; and consequently what emerges among black men (blue- and white-collar) who are steady providers is the family form (Figure 4.1) that has predominated in most other segments of industrial society up to this time.[101] This form, in varying degrees, has been emerging around the world as societies modernize, regardless of skin color, geography, political ideology, or whatever.[102]

Some black men and women believe that the black women's search for male-female equality at this time undercuts efforts of the black man to gain some modicum of equality with the white man. As Amina Baraka (Mrs. LeRoi Jones) puts it:

> First things first. The black movement is the most important movement to us. . . . The black woman's roles . . . [are] to inspire our men, educate our children and participate in the social development of our [black] nation. . . .[103]

Compounding the matter still further for blacks is the matrifocal family form that has persisted for so long in lower-class black society, owing to economic discrimination against black men. The call for sex equality may seem unreal to lower-class blacks who have experienced substantial female power, chiefly because the male had no resources from which to bargain for status or power. Even among stable black families above the lower-class there is evidence of greater female power and more

99. Norton, p. 355.
100. There is no necessary contradiction between black power and individual achievement. *See* Scanzoni, 1971, chapter eight.
101. *Ibid.*
102. *See* Goode, 1963, *passim.*
103. King, p. 75.

equality than exists among white families at comparable status levels.[104] Furthermore, some black men are trying to make black women feel guilty about the long-standing matrifocal pattern and telling them that if they truly wish to rid themselves of guilt, they ought to accept the belief that the "superiority and dominance of the male is the most 'natural' and 'normal' relationship." [105]

On one side, therefore, some blacks believe that anything that siphons off energies from improving the position of black men, and thus their women with them, ought to be relegated to a very low priority. On the other side some black Feminists feel that "black liberation" is not negated by "female liberation," or vice-versa.[106] Beal claims, "It is fallacious reasoning that in order for the black man to be strong, the black woman has to be weak." [107] She claims that for blacks to attain their goals "we need our whole army out there dealing with the enemy, and not half an army. . . . To assign women the role of housekeeper and mother while men go forth into battle is a highly questionable doctrine for a revolutionary to maintain." [108] She condemns the inequalitarian implications of the model described in Figure 4.1, and instead, both she and Norton call for equality in marriage based on black women being occupationally involved as "competent teachers, doctors, . . . political scientists, etc. . . . Black women sitting at home reading bedtime stories to their children are just not going to make it." [109]

Beal, furthermore, observes that while black men are indeed economically discriminated against, their annual median incomes are higher than those of white women workers, and that black women are the most poorly paid of all workers in our society. In 1967, for instance, government figures indicate a median income for white male workers of $6,704; black males, $4,277; white females, $3,991; black females, $2,861.[110] Lower-class black women, with no male present but with several children, are the poorest of all the American poor.

An additional complication is the issue of childbearing. Black Feminists tend to argue in favor of contraception and abortion for blacks, and the legal adoption by blacks of the great numbers of black children already alive and currently living in orphanages.[111] There is an ideological and a pragmatic reason for this position. Ideologically, they, as all

104. Blood and Wolfe; Scanzoni, 1971, chapter six.
105. La Rue, p. 63; Beal, p. 343; Murray, pp. 89ff.
106. Beal, p. 343; La Rue, p. 64.
107. Beal, p. 344.
108. *Ibid.*, pp. 344, 353.
109. *Ibid.*, pp. 344–45. *See also* Norton.
110. Beal, p. 345.
111. La Rue, p. 64.

Feminists, resist the notion that the "ideal woman" is a mother gently nurturing the many young that flock 'round her knee.[112] Pragmatically, they argue that a great part of the severe economic burden of lower-class black women is, in fact, the large numbers of children they are forced to support, often alone. They are concerned that these women are unable to prepare their children adequately to meet the demands of industrial society.[113] On the other hand, some blacks praise traditional motherhood and see it as the highest goal for black women.[114] Moreover, these persons argue, child limitation is another of "Whitey's" techniques (close to genocide) to keep down the number of black people and thus minimize their political power. The more blacks there are, it is reasoned, the better off the (black) nation will be.

It is not certain just how, in the foreseeable future, attempts toward sex equality will affect attempts at race equality, and vice-versa, within black society. Two things, however, should be kept in mind as we move next into discussion of role-equality within marriage. First, as noted above, there is some evidence to indicate that at present there is greater egalitarianism among black than among white marriages. Second, black Feminists seem to concur among themselves that one of the goals they seek is a marital structure different from that described in Figure 4.1. "On the road to equality," says Norton, "there is no better place for blacks to detour around American values than in foregoing its example in the treatment of its women and the organization of its family life." [115]

CHANGE IN THE FUTURE STRUCTURE OF MARRIAGE

There are at least two highly industrialized nations which provide an empirical basis for comparison, against which to make *relatively* sound projections regarding the future of family change in the United States. These are Sweden and the Soviet Union. Sweden, according to Dahlström, remains "an essentially capitalistic system." [116] Though socialist parties have controlled the parliament for some time, and though Sweden has evolved a high degree of state welfare, the control of business and industry remains in private hands. In Russia, of course, business and industry are in the hands of government which, in turn, is controlled by the Communist Party.

Skolnick and Skolnick claim that most modern nations have already

112. *Ibid.*
113. "Statement on Birth Control," Morgan, 1970, pp. 360–61.
114. *See* King, 1971.
115. Norton, p. 356.
116. Dahlström, p. 174.

entered a "postindustrial, post-Protestant ethic" era.[117] However, it is misleading to associate "postindustrial" with "post-Protestant ethic." As coined by Bell, the former term describes a country in which "the weight of the economy has shifted from the product sector to services. . . ."[118] Instead of most people being employed in producing material goods, more and more people become involved in *service* to others—whether in foods, leisure, repair, education, welfare, public service, and so on.

At the same time, a postindustrial society must have a firm industrial base—it is an affluent society in the extreme. But this setting in no way diminishes or negates a work and achievement ethic, whatever its origin. There is every evidence that a strong work ethic remains in our society.[119] Indeed, pressures to open up the society to blacks, working-class children, and women, and pressures to industrialize the third world mean that this ethic is actually being extended within the United States and worldwide. Talk of our becoming a leisure society is, according to Wilensky, more fanciful than real.[120] While it may be true that certain blue-collar workers need to labor fewer hours than formerly, it is the blue-collar jobs that are eliminated in an automated, postindustrial setting. On the other hand, as more and more persons become involved in professional, technical, and service occupations, they will find themselves part of that "growing minority of the . . . labor force . . . who usually work 55 hours a week or more. . . ."[121]

The value placed on work is not intrinsically white, nor male, nor Western, nor middle-class. In premodern society, it emerges obviously out of the need for survival. In modernizing or modern societies, it emerges, in addition, out of the requirement that the most important tasks be filled by the most talented persons. The incentive to get talented persons into these slots, and to get them to perform well, is through a higher reward level (tangible and intangible) than for less "functionally significant" slots. To illustrate: whether a factory be in New York, Moscow, Accra, Buenos Aires, or Tokyo, the manager of that factory is more critical to its survival than the janitor on the night shift. The manager, therefore, is rewarded more highly, not just materially but also in prestige and power —in the exercise of leadership, responsibility, and creativity in planning, in developing his own ideas and testing them out, in his freedom to innovate—in short, to experience self-fulfillment and "self-actualization" in work that is "absorbing and satisfying." [122]

117. Skolnick and Skolnick, p. 30.
118. Bell, 1967, pp. 643–44.
119. *See* Wilensky, 1966.
120. *Ibid.*
121. *Ibid.*, p. 125.
122. Figes, p. 91.

Therefore, work, achievement, differential rewards, and differential social status flowing from these rewards promise to be around for a long time, even within postindustrial society—regardless if it be capitalist, socialist, or communist. Indeed, if Mitchell is correct: "the main thrust of any [women's] emancipation movement must still concentrate on the economic element—the entry of women fully into public industry," [123] then it is essential that the labor force be continually expanding worldwide. The advanced, postindustrial nations provide more opportunities for women than the less modernized, because to the extent that they are service-oriented, brains rather than brawn clearly become the chief criterion for recruitment and rewards.

But what about those younger persons—usually students, white, mostly male, from upper-middle class homes—who have "tuned out" occupational achievement, and the success theme? Many such persons live in communal settings, and they see no value at all in educational and occupational attainments for *either* sex. They are part of the "green revolution" or a counterculture which defines

> itself in diametric opposition to some of the basic values of bourgeois society . . . the "Protestant ethic"—discipline, achievement and faith in the onward and upward thrust of technological society. These same values are now perceived as "repression" and "hypocrisy," and the very promises of technological society are rejected as illusionary or downright immoral. A hedonistic ethic is proclaimed . . . designed to liberate the individual from the bourgeois inhibitions. . . . Achievement is perceived as futility and "alienation," its ethos as "uptight" and . . . inimical to life. Implied in all this is a radical aversion to capitalism. . . . [The movement's radicalism] is not simply in opposition to . . . bourgeois capitalism but to the very idea of technological society. The . . . imagery of salvation is intensely bucolic, the troops of the revolution are not the toiling masses of the Marxist prophecy but naked children of nature dancing to the tune of primitive drums.[124]

Berger and Berger note that the percentages of young people who have totally embraced the green, or cultural, revolution, is statistically insignificant. For example, interviews with a national probability sample of college graduates, conducted in May, 1971, revealed that the average annual income (men and women, graduates and undergraduates) expected just one year after college was $9,000. Their expected average annual salary after ten years was over $18,000.[125] These data hardly support the

123. Mitchell, p. 171.
124. Berger and Berger, p. 21.
125. Unidex Corporation, Bloomington, Indiana. Bloomington *Herald–Telephone*, June 16, 1971.

notion that at present more than a tiny minority of white (or black) college students have any idea of tuning out of modern society and its material benefits, to say nothing of more than half of American youth who never even get to college.[126]

But the Bergers' more critical point is that in the foreseeable future it will make no difference whatsoever to the continuity of modern, technological societies if even a substantial number of white, highly privileged young *men* do tune out. The continued expansion (discussed below) of technological societies means that new positions plus older, vacated ones formerly filled by privileged men, but now disdained by them, will have to be filled by others. The Bergers call this a "sociological windfall" for "the newly college educated children of the lower-middle and working classes." [127] Women *and* men from these groups will fill these slots, as will black women and men, and so will many upper-middle-class white women who, heretofore, have never had the opportunities for achievement that some of their "own men" are coming to disdain. The Bergers describe this process as the "blueing of America," i.e., the formerly less-privileged groups gaining the opportunities voluntarily relinquished by the once more-privileged. The more upper-middle-class white men reject the achievement syndrome, the more opportunities there will be for all other persons to participate in the syndrome more fully than ever before. Thus, in the years immediately before us the green revolution may actually supply added stimulus to Feminist goals by removing from the scene many of the sons of fathers who currently control most of the valued job positions, and who, in the past, have succeeded their fathers but now no longer choose to get into their father's "bag."

According to Oppenheimer, perhaps the most significant demographic reason why so many American wives have gone to work since 1940 was the great demand for female labor when it was in short supply during a period of great economic expansion.[128] The percentage of all wives who are in the paid labor force and living with their husbands has risen from about 15 percent in 1940 to 23 percent in 1952, to 37 percent in 1968.[129] On the basis of her "estimates and projections of demand and supply for the 1969–2000 period," she sees "women at all stages of the family life cycle . . . coming to work in ever greater numbers." [130] As they do this, she predicts:

126. *Current Population Reports,* P–20, No. 222, pp. 1–4.
127. Berger and Berger, p. 22.
128. Oppenheimer, 1970.
129. *Current Population Reports,* P–60, No. 64, p. 1.
130. Oppenheimer, pp. 13–14.

It is inevitable that many are going to stop viewing work as a brief inter-
lude in a long life devoted to their families. Instead, they will start to
consider work a possible lifetime activity, interrupted at times, perhaps,
but nevertheless one of their major adult roles.[131]

Hence, in the future we can expect ever more married women to work
—many still in low-paying "female jobs," motivated mostly by a desire
to boost family life style, but on a more permanent basis than has been
true heretofore. We can expect more women, in short, to occupy the
status of *junior partner* who are yet unable to bargain for genuine *equal
partner* status with their husbands since their inputs into the marriage
generally remain less than those of their husbands:

> However, if female jobs are unattractive to *male* workers with their long-
> range commitment to work, how are *female* workers going to start feeling
> about such jobs as women's involvement in the labor force becomes ever
> more extensive? Will they continue to be satisfied with what used to be
> good enough for an interim activity? For as long as work was of secondary
> importance, then women's work goals remained limited and the character-
> istics of women's jobs that make them most unattractive to men—poor pay
> and poor advancement opportunities—did not cause a great deal of dis-
> satisfaction. However, as their work becomes more important to women
> . . . then the more irritating will become the poor pay and the lack of
> opportunities. . . . women's changing work *behavior* will inevitably affect
> women's attitudes toward work.[132]

Oppenheimer's point is that in the next few decades as more women
get more education and work more years, they will develop a sense of
class consciousness, i.e., that they are in fact being discriminated against
in the labor force. This sense of things, in conjunction with the ideology
of historic and current Feminism that women *should* be equal with
men, could very likely lead increasing numbers of women to define
work in terms of occupational achievement that is geared toward the
most significant slots and rewarded in generous fashion. Women will
do this not to copy or be like men, for there is nothing inherently masculine about occupational achievement behavior, any more than it is
inherently white or black. They will behave this way because they seek
directly the rewards offered by modern occupational structures, and
in order to obtain them they must behave as any other *person* (regardless of sex or race) and conform to their demands.

Collective disapproval of a situation is far more effective in changing

131. *Ibid.*
132. *Ibid.*, pp. 13–14.

it than the resentment of a lone individual.[133] As more and more women develop an ever keener sense of injustice about job discrimination, they will collectively enter into conflict with those males who control the economic, political, and legal institutions. Already groups of women have brought, and won, several court suits against employers who have been guilty of economic discrimination. More collective political and legal action of all sorts is to be expected in the future, as women (analogous to black power—blacks acting in concert politically and economically), develop "woman power."

But what are the consequences of these shifts in role-structure for conjugal marriage? Where role-*specialization* now prevails in most families, the future promises the increasing frequency of role-*interchangeability*. The husband, in many cases, will no longer be the *unique provider;* the wife will no longer be the *unique homemaker.* Because many wives will become as career-oriented as husbands, and because their education, job status, and incomes will be roughly equal, wives will be able to bargain for equal status and power in marriage. But in order to moderate our concept of how extensively and how rapidly the shift from role-specialization to role-interchangeability might occur in the United States, we need to look at the examples of Sweden and the Soviet Union.

Sweden

It is understandable how in the kibbutz, role-interchangeability eventually became submerged under the demands of an agricultural setting in which brawn was so significant. But what of highly industrialized Sweden? Feminism never evaporated there as it did in the U.S. in the early years of the twentieth century.[134] Swedish advocates of Feminism considered unfair the pattern of marital structure portrayed in Figures 2.1, 2.2, and 4.1, and entered into serious conflict with those men who wished to maintain it. This conflict over the rules of the game was probably carried out both at the institutional and the micro levels of individual marriages. Nevertheless, this basic conflict has not resulted in widespread marital dissolution in Sweden. Sweden's crude divorce rate is lower than that of the United States, where far more traditionalism in sex roles prevails.

Instead, it seems that one result of this conflict has been to place Swedish wives in a situation of greater advantage and power than wives in the United States. While Swedish women have by no means gained full equality of resources and power with Swedish men, it is now *official*

133. Blau, p. 23.
134. O'Neill, 1969.

government policy to bring about genuine *equality* between the sexes. To achieve this goal what is the ". . . radical change in deep-rooted traditions and attitudes [that] must be brought among both women and men . . . ?" [135]

> The view that women ought to be economically supported by marriage must be effectively refuted . . . as this view is a direct obstacle to the economic independence of women and their ability to compete on equal terms in the labour market. Similarly, the husband's traditional obligation to support his wife must be modified to constitute a responsibility, shared with her, for the support of the children. [136]

In 1966, in Sweden, most employed men worked forty-five or more hours per week. Fifty-five percent of employed married women worked one to thirty-four hours weekly. [137] Moreover, as in the United States, employed women with children under seven years of age worked significantly fewer hours per week than did married women of similar ages without children. [138] Likewise, Swedish women are relegated to feminine jobs, just as elsewhere: they make up the great bulk of dental assistants, nurses, hospital lab assistants, private nurses, receptionists; and they make up 90 percent of all clerks. [139] In sum, compared to men, fewer Swedish women work; those who are employed work fewer hours; they work in lower-status jobs; they earn less and obtain less prestige and power. [140] Thus in spite of official policy to the contrary and many gains during the sixties, [141] Swedish working women remain second-class employees as they are so far in every industrialized society. [142]

It does not appear, therefore, that the kind of widespread class consciousness that Oppenheimer predicts will emerge in the United States has yet emerged among the bulk of Swedish women workers. This lack of resources and bargaining power is subsequently reflected in marital role-structure. While most observers concur that there is greater equality and role-interchangeability among Swedish than American marriages, traditional role-specialization nevertheless persists among most Swedish marriages. [143] Men remain *chiefly* responsible for occupational, women for domestic duties.

135. Sandlund, p. 5.
136. *Ibid.*
137. Dahlström, p. 109.
138. *Ibid.*, p. 111.
139. *Ibid.*, p. 115.
140. *Ibid.*
141. Liljeström, p. 214.
142. Dahlström, p. 133.
143. *Ibid.*; also Liljeström.

Soviet Union

What about Russia, where an essentially totalitarian state has more power than a democratic society to enforce policies based on Marxist ideology regarding sex equality? First, far more women work in the Soviet Union than in almost any other modern nation: 70 percent overall; 80 percent among women ages twenty to thirty-nine, the childbearing period.[144] An important pressure that moves women to work is the low wages that most Russian men earn: "a single paycheck provides only a bare subsistence." [145] Also, "government and party action has altered social custom and public attitudes toward the employment of women. . . . Few fields are considered inaccessible, and a woman is actually likely to feel defensive if she does not have a job. The regime has been particularly successful in opening the fields of science and technology to women." [146] The extensive legal provisions and executive orders seeking to remove discrimination have been strictly applied and enforced.[147]

Over the last few decades, as Russia sought to modernize very rapidly, especially in science and technology, it sought to attract the best talent possible irrespective of sex to these significant slots. Yet "the choice of a specific field of study is not decided by the state. The percentage of men and women enrolled in each discipline is a fairly faithful reflection of the relative attraction of a field." [148] As a result, women make up 60 percent of those studying chemical engineering, hydrology, meteorology, geodesy, and cartography; 75 percent of those studying the technology of food and consumer-goods production; 20 percent of those studying mining engineering, transportation, and machine building; and 53 percent of medical and 25 percent of agricultural students. "In comparison with other countries . . . these are strikingly high percentages." [149]

Likewise, Soviet women are represented far more in the professions than American women: 75 percent of all medical doctors in the Soviet Union are women, compared with only 7 percent in America. Thirty-three percent of all engineers in Russia are women, compared to 1 percent in America; for college professors, the comparison is 35 percent to 22 percent; and so on.[150] Nevertheless, 80 percent of all Soviet working women are engaged in heavy, unskilled, physical labor—in many cases

144. Dodge, p. 239.
145. *Ibid.*, p. 240.
146. *Ibid.*
147. *Ibid.*; Dahlström, p. 182.
148. Dodge, p. 242.
149. *Ibid.*
150. *Ibid.*, p. 244.

agricultural: "field workers, and livestock tenders, while men handle the skilled mechanical and construction work and serve as administrators."[151] And once in the professions, Soviet women suffer much the same kinds of discrimination that women do in other modern societies: less advancement, slower promotion, less responsibility, less power, and smaller salaries than men.[152]

How do these factors affect role-specialization or interchangeability in Soviet marriages? We saw in chapter one that one result of the government's attempt to *enforce* sex-role equality has been a very high rate of divorce—currently the highest in the world. The demands for change were imposed so rapidly and with such stringency that men could not assimilate them—indeed, they continue to resist them strongly.[153] According to Field, "Soviet men, jealous of their masculinity and spoiled by their indulgent, strong mothers and submissive sisters, refuse to help their wives in household duties."[154] Field comments that Soviet women are responsible for purchasing all the family's daily consumption needs, and due to very poor retail facilities, it takes several hours each day.[155] Poor housing conditions make domestic duties exceedingly complicated and time-consuming.[156] Add to these responsibilities those connected with child care, and we find that most working women there, as elsewhere, have nowhere near actual marital-role equality. In part, the continued inequality is owing to the fact that in spite of Marxist ideology and official laws to the contrary, "economic support of the family," according to Geiger, "has continued to be primarily the man's task."[157] Even in Russia, the husband is still defined as *the unique provider*. And when we consider the persisting discrimination against employed Russian wives, we conclude that many of them, like their counterparts elsewhere, lack resources adequate to bargain for equal-partner status. Thus in the great majority of Soviet marriages role-interchangeability remains the exception that proves the rule.

According to Bronfenbrenner, however, there is one relatively recent trend that may considerably stimulate greater role-interchangeability in many Soviet marriages. It is an innovation that Sweden had once pursued and thereafter ignored for a time and is only now once again reviving.[158] In 1956 and again in 1959, Premier Khrushchev proposed to

151. *Ibid.*, p. 243.
152. *Ibid.*, p. 244.
153. Geiger.
154. Field, p. 22.
155. *Ibid.*, p. 22.
156. *Ibid.*
157. Geiger, p. 241.
158. Kelman, p. 22.

his government "the possibility of educating all children in boarding schools. . . . Millions of women will be released from the household chores of child-rearing. . . ."[159] By 1960, 10 percent of all Soviet children under two years of age were placed voluntarily by their parents in these boarding schools.[160] For children between three and six years of age, the figure is "18 percent or higher."[161] Also undertaken was an extensive program of building "prolonged-day" schools which differ from the boarding schools only in that "children go home at seven in the evening and return the next morning at eight o'clock."[162]

Soviet educators told Bronfenbrenner that by 1970, one-third of all school children would be enrolled in *both* types of new schools, and that sometime during the 1980s the figure would probably reach 100 percent.[163] There has been no official pressure on Russian parents to send their children to these schools. However, because of the crowded conditions under which so many families are forced to live, plus the limited intellectual stimulation and material advantages that most parents can give to their children, they are only too happy to cooperate with the government. By this means, parents believe children receive many more opportunities for enrichment and achievement than they could possibly give them by keeping them in traditional surroundings.[164]

It is obvious that if trends toward urban, communal upbringing of children continue, substantial impediments to occupational achievement will have been removed for Soviet wives and mothers. Nonetheless, it should be made clear that most Russians do not see the new schools as "removing" their children from them. In both types of new settings, but especially in the day-care facilities, parents maintain close contact with their children and value them, as do Western parents, for the rewards their children can give them—both expressive and instrumental in the vicarious enjoyment of their children's attainments.[165] At present, therefore, the structure of Soviet marriage is in gradual transition. In slightly more than five decades, it has shifted from a strongly patriarchal arrangement into one in which many wives, though still subordinate to husbands in most instances, are gaining increasing entry into the occupational pursuits that provide the resources to enable them to bargain more effectively for equal status and power. Furthermore, if trends continue toward developing extensive facilities that relieve wives of

159. Bronfenbrenner, p. 109.
160. *Ibid.*, p. 110.
161. *Ibid.*
162. *Ibid.*, p. 111.
163. *Ibid.*
164. *Ibid.*, pp. 111–12.
165. *Ibid.*, pp. 113–16.

many of the tedious responsibilities of child care, then we may expect, first, more and more Soviet women becoming very well educated and highly trained and developing "modern" role-conceptions of themselves in terms of occupational pursuits. Second, because of these cumulative sets of factors, greater numbers of Soviet wives will likely pursue occupations and careers and thus gain a stronger bargaining position with husbands than they possess even at present.

ROLE-INTERCHANGEABILITY, SATISFACTION WITH MARRIAGE, AND MARITAL STABILITY

If the above projections are correct, and the Scandinavian countries and the Soviet Union are gradually moving towards role-definitions of wives as coproviders with husbands, and if the United States and most other modern nations are also slowly moving in the same direction, what can we say to describe specifically: (1) the nature of this significant change towards marital role-interchangeability; and (2) its consequences for marital satisfactions and stability?

First, we should note that the examples of Russia, Sweden, the kibbutz, and so on, where there have been attempts at long-lasting and substantial innovations in marital structure, give no hint whatsoever of any departure from the general pattern of *monogamy* by more than a handful of persons. Hence, whatever *significant* changes in family forms occur in the *foreseeable* future in Western society, they will probably be contained within a monogamous framework. There has been covert, extramarital sex since recorded history, and whether "affairs" (as opposed to overt "swinging") will increase or decline in the future, no one can yet tell. It is quite clear, however, that monogamy can, as it always has, exist alongside traditional forms of covert extramarital sex. However, the available evidence suggests that few Americans would prefer to *change* their marital patterns to legitimize *covert* adultery.[166] Secretive behavior of this sort appears to be a severe challenge to the current fundamental rules of the marriage game, and when one partner challenges these rules it usually spells the dissolution of the marriage.[167]

A second point is the quest for *utopia* in marriage patterns, which by definition can never exist on this earth. As we saw, many critics of contemporary marriage argue that it is unworkable, untenable, and stifling to individual development. They, along with Feminists who contend for family experiments or sex equality, believe that the future

166. Neubeck, 1969, p. 48.
167. Johnson, p. 49.

could hold better and happier marriages than at present, if only certain changes are made.

Unfortunately, the definitions of "better" and "happier" are extremely elusive. Did persons experience better family life prior to widespread industrialization, as Ariés seems to imply, when there were intimate ties and substantial interlocking between persons who were active participants of both conjugal and blood kin groups? [168] Is family life better in Sweden and the Soviet Union than it is in the United States? Will it be better in the future if Western societies follow their lead toward role-interchangeability or toward other experimental family forms? Whatever the answers to these questions, one thing is certain—there never has been, nor will there ever be, any family form that is free from its own types of conflicts, tensions, burdens, difficulties, and problems. Hence, although future forms that evolve may shed old burdens, they are sure to take on new ones. This, of course, is the essence of any social structure, i.e., that perceived dissatisfactions, injustices, and conflicts give rise to change and to new patterns, which inevitably generate their own dissatisfactions, and so the cycle of "regenerative force" and "new vitality" become "the basis of [ongoing] social reorganization." [169]

For instance, let us assume that increasing numbers of women, worldwide, seek to move along the continuum from junior partner to equal partner. It is clear that only if women themselves actively seek the status of equal partner will it ever be achieved, just as they themselves had to seek a shift from their *property* status to the statuses they now hold. Males (as we shall document below) are not about to upset the status quo that provides them with such a favorable position in the current family structure.

Currently, males have maximum freedom to pursue highly valued occupational behavior. Work, as we saw, remains in modern society the chief means to gain a sense of moral worth, to validate one's self in the eyes of significant others. Most males in our society would suffer severe disapproval if they should happen to choose a role such as "househusband" and reject occupational endeavors. In fact, this is a moot point. Within the foreseeable future, it seems safe to say that few males will drop out entirely of highly valued occupational pursuits to engage in what an increasing number of females themselves term as household drudgery.

At the same time, most wives currently have minimum freedom to

168. Ariés, pp. 365ff.
169. Blau, p. 301.

pursue occupational achievement with the same degree of commitment as their husbands. They are locked in to domestic pursuits. Yet it is already apparent that a growing minority of educated women are coming to demand, as their right, the serious pursuit of occupational achievement with *the same amount of freedom* and commitment that males currently possess. This includes the same freedom to be mobile socially, occupationally, and geographically that husbands have. It is not probable, however, that many of their husbands, though they too are likely to be well-educated, will see this much freedom as legitimate, *precisely because it will be costly—it will tend to limit their freedom to pursue their own occupations.*

To take a mundane though very real example, let us assume both marital partners are seriously pursuing occupational careers in, say, Chicago. Let us also assume that the husband receives an attractive job offer from Los Angeles (whether he be businessman, clergyman, engineer, professor, or whatever), or is asked by his present organization to move there to accept a promotion. But if the wife moves with her husband, it may very well be that such a move would seriously hamper her own career. To complicate the situation further by an equally real possibility, what if at that very same time she is asked by her own firm to transfer to New York, or she receives a job offer from there? Or, what if, at some other time, when her husband cannot, or does not want to move at all, she feels that a move would be beneficial to her occupational pursuits? Bargaining over these issues could easily turn into basic conflict and become extraordinary threatening to the stability of their marriage.

Up to this time, there is evidence that even married professional women have tended to follow their husbands when they move, and not to expect their husbands to move on their account. A study of women dentists, for example, revealed it was "normative" for them to give up their practices and to change cities whenever their husbands changed jobs.[170] For these women, the study showed that this meant considerable sacrifice and cost in licensing, equipment, and time required to build a clientele. Yet Linn reports that this procedure was accepted by both husbands and wives, and that neither sex gave any indication that husbands might ever in turn "allow" wives to influence their choice of geographic location. As we have defined the various statuses that modern wives may occupy, even that tiny minority of American women who are professionals continue to occupy the marital status of junior partner. But what of the future?

170. Linn, 1971.

Certain observers have speculated that future divorce trends may slacken somewhat because more people are becoming more economically advantaged.[171] Such predictions are based on a model of marriage such as seen in Figure 4.1. As applied to the bulk of the population the predictions may be valid, at the same time that the marriages of the highly educated may face greater levels of conflict over basic rules than ever before. This may result in several related trends: (1) a higher rate of divorce among that segment of the urban population whose rates are currently lowest (men with highest education); (2) a reversal of the present trends toward decreased female singleness. It is already the case that of all women, those who are the most educated are the most likely to remain single.[172] It is clear that there will be more highly educated women in the future, and that many of them will be aware of the *potential* basic conflict that the presence of two achievers introduces into marriage. Consequently, many of them may not marry at all until they can find a male with whom they could achieve consensus over geographic mobility in particular, and the whole dual-achiever pattern in general; and since it is likely that for some years there will be relatively few such males, these women will either marry late or else remain single.

In those marriages where some sort of consensus is reached over the dual-achiever syndrome, the husband would no longer be defined as unique provider. In effect, these equal partners would both be providers in an *interchangeable* sense. Referring back to the dynamics of Figure 4.1 (wife defined as complement or junior partner) we saw that the husband exchanges the status and economic benefits he provides to his wife for expressive rewards, deference, and conjugal solidarity. If, in the future, he is no longer able to provide these resources in a *unique* fashion, *what are the basic processes which then account for feelings of solidarity, cohesion, and which lead to marital stability?* May we therefore expect more marital instability among the better educated, owing not only to negative conflict over wife's achievements, but also because they are less bound together—less interdependent—than were the partners in marriages based on role-specialization?

The entertainment industry provides a vivid illustration of this issue. Perhaps more than in any other single occupation, that industry supplies women with significant income, prestige, and some degree of influence and power. Undoubtedly for many women on stage and in movies, rewards are based on purely physical and sexual attributes. Yet

171. Parke and Glick, p. 250.
172. Carter and Glick, p. 310.

many others possess genuine talent in acting, singing, and dancing and have been recognized and rewarded generously for their achievements.[173] These achievements, in many cases, have given them equal or even superior resources with which to bargain with their husbands for marital status and power. If a woman is a talented actress who commands a large salary and considerable prestige, does she then give in to her husband simply because he is a man, and the head of the home and, since for efficiency's sake *someone* has to make final decisions, should *he* not make them? And who should decide on competing job demands that call for her to be on location in Europe and for him at the same time to work in Hollywood?

While perhaps personality factors play a large role in the marital relationships of those in the entertainment industry, the fact that those wives have access to resources which potentially can make them co-providers and equal partners with their husbands must also certainly play a part in the apparent instability of many entertainment marriages. This industry is the first occupational group that women have "invaded" and men have not fled, compared, say, to library science or elementary school teaching. Yet when married to these highly achievement-oriented women, many men resist relinquishing traditional male rights and privileges, and consequently, the outcome is often separation and divorce.

Thus, in the short run, as more and more highly trained women become more and more achievement-oriented and enter a wider range of careers and professions, we might expect higher rates of marital instability than at present among the more advantaged population groups. Nevertheless, we could predict that the structure of the current processes of husband-wife reciprocity may gradually alter to accommodate these new female role-rights.

Over a century ago John Stuart Mill contended that just as there are genuinely equal partners in a two-person business enterprise, so this arrangement can exist in marriage as well.[174] In such a business situation, the participants are generally equal investors in the enterprise. On the basis of this equal resource provision, they have roughly equal power in bargaining with each other on policy matters. Besides equality in decision-making, there is also equality in profit-sharing. What is always kept foremost is the good of the group and the good of both partners—meaning that both the enterprise and its partners should make profits. This overriding goal means that the partners will play virtually

173. Though they have generally been excluded from positions as directors, producers, etc.
174. Mill, 1869, pp. 472ff.

any role in the enterprise necessary to achieve it. Though role-specialization (and relative degree of importance to the business) may evolve, it is not permanently fixed nor based on ascribed characteristics of the partners. Furthermore, they may shift roles or alter their structure substantially. All of this flexibility and potential interchangeability is for one chief reason—the mutual enjoyment of maximum profits.

As this analogy applies to the marriage group it means that some Neofeminists may seek (through bargaining or conflict) the following kinds of changes. Currently, the good of the marriage and both its partners is defined in terms of profits (prestige, money) achieved *directly* by the husband and transmitted to the wife, who thus receives them *indirectly*. In the future, the good of the marriage may come to be defined as one in which *both* partners achieve these profits *directly*. Many wives, perhaps, will simply refuse to accept the notion that their good is being served through *indirect* participation in the profit-making process and will instead seek *direct* participation. In those marriages, therefore, where this kind of role structure becomes the basis of consensus, or the rules of the game, Figure 4.1 would need to be modified to look instead something like Figure 5.1.

Fig. 5.1 Husband–Wife Role Reciprocity Based on Equal–Partner Status and Provider–Role Interchangeability

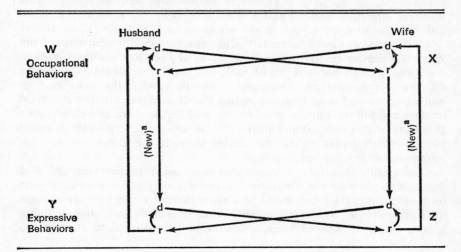

a Compared to Figure 4.1.

First, the wife's instrumental role (X_d) no longer includes chief responsibility for household tasks, nor the *obligation* to defer to her husband's wishes because of his unique resource provision. Decision-making and performance of household tasks (including number and spacing of children and child care) become issues to be settled through ongoing bargaining and conflict processes.

Second, she (X_d) now shares equally in the responsibility to supply status and economic resources to the conjugal unit. While these kinds of role-redefinitions may boggle the minds of some white males and be deemed chaotic by some blacks because of their desire to affirm male authority and leadership through a unique provider role, such redefinitions are, nonetheless, a structural requisite if the marriage is to be described as a genuine equal-partner situation as described in Mill's analogy.

Third, and concomitant, is the redefinition of (W_d)—the husband now *shares* the responsibility to achieve; it is no longer uniquely his. Fourth, it now becomes his right (W_r) to receive socioeconomic benefits from his wife, just as it continues to be her right (X_r) to receive such from him. In short, *the X and W poles are defined in exactly the same fashion for husbands and wives as for our two hypothetical business partners.*

Fifth, there is now an arrow from W_r to Y_d where there was none in Figure 4.1. To the degree that the husband perceives his status and economic rights being met, he then feels motivated to perform his expressive duties—to behave positively to his wife with companionship, physical affection, and empathy. The wife behaves in similar fashion, only this continues the pattern already given in Figure 4.1 $(X_r$ to $Z_d)$.

Sixth, what is now substantially different for her is a new arrow from Z_r to X_d, similar to the arrow from Y_r to W_d for her husband. Hence, the more the expressive rights of *each*, not just the husband as in Figure 4.1, are met (as well as status and economic rights), the more *each* is motivated to maintain ongoing occupational achievement for the good of the unit, for the mutual good of one another, and for any children.[175] It is only at this point that Figure 2.2D becomes a reality—wife as *equal partner*—with equal rights and duties at both the expressive *and* instrumental dimensions of marriage.

One could, therefore, suggest that with *each* partner obliged and desirous to provide the maximum levels of status and economic inputs to the marriage, the result could be a more extensive and intensive system of husband-wife reciprocities, with the ultimate consequence being greater levels of expressiveness, cohesion, and stability than exist in the

---

175. *See* p. 159 below for further discussion of exchange and specialization between equals.

present pattern of role-specialization, where only the male is obliged to play the provider role (*see* pp. 159ff.). Moreover, in the present marital pattern, the situation of a male becoming incapacitated and unable to work, or being laid off and unable to find a job tends to have serious negative consequences for husband-wife reciprocity and cohesion.[176] Such crises would not be so significantly negative, however, if both partners in the marriage were defined as legitimate coproviders.

The opposite argument may also hold—namely that serious rivalries may occur at any time within that kind of marriage (just as in a business) and may result in much higher levels of dissolution among higher-status families than is the case now. We know, for example, that the more education women get the less likely they are to be divorced, at least up through four years of college.[177] But when women (white and especially nonwhite) obtain more education than four years of college (probably the most achievement-oriented women), they become the most likely of *all* American women to be divorced and not remarried.[178]

Thinking back to our discussion of Bamenda women, there is clearly a close congruence between the economic resources, power, and equality they hold in an agrarian setting, and the model just described as it applies to modern society. The resources that give wives equality and power in modern society are not, however, linked to the land nor to physical brawn. Instead, the supply of resources is the same as it is for husbands —strong commitment to and full and effective participation in the opportunity structure. The degree of participation and its inevitable consequences for marital structure is, of course, at the heart of male-female conflict—at the macro level as competing interest groups—and increasingly at the micro level, between particular husbands and wives such as the hypothetical Frenches.

The Great Debate

In Scandinavia and the Soviet Union, as well as in the United States, there is much explicit debate about the feasibility of changes in marital structure, based on genuine role-equality that emanates from equal access to career opportunity. On the one side, Ford contends that:

> It does not seem likely that changes in technology or conscious striving for an equality of the sexes with respect to the roles they play will make any really fundamental changes in the foreseeable future. Many theorists . . . tend to underestimate biological factors and their implications for social life. Men are male and women are female in their basic capacities

176. *See* Bakke.
177. Carter and Glick, p. 257.
178. *Ibid.*

and characteristics. . . . Technology . . . appears to have its limitations in equalizing the roles that each sex will play. . . .[179]

Ford's point, that there is something innately different about the sexes which points them to different life spheres and which inevitably generates inequality, is only partly modified by Margaret Mead who in a discussion of future sex-role patterns suggests that:

> The education of girls, especially in regard to career expectations . . . would still differ from that of boys. Girls would be directed toward occupations that were related to nurture, teaching, comforting, and curing; they would be expected to devise their basic life satisfactions from their contributions to the achievement of others. The two sexes would still be socially typed as complementary. . . . The model . . . would probably continue to be one based on an achieving husband and a wife who was primarily concerned with support and the daily care of bodily and psychological needs.[180]

Mead, in effect, argues that the model of Figure 4.1 will continue to predominate, though with more and more women becoming junior partners less restricted to the home, but continuing to engage in nurturant or "feminine" occupation. When we shift to the other side of the debate, we find that D'Andrade concludes that in most cultures "males are more sexually active, more dominant, more deferred to, more aggressive, less responsible, less nurturant, and less emotionally expressive than females." [181] He notes, however, that in some cultures the differences do not exist at all and in some (e.g., the Bamendas) "the trend is actually reversed." [182] He then makes the point which has been reiterated throughout this chapter—and indeed the whole book—the point which is the key to changes in future marital patterns: "these differences [in dominance and aggressiveness] are related to and presumably influenced by which sex controls economic capital. . . ." [183]

Coming full circle from Ford, Grønseth argues that not only is what he calls the "Husband Economic Provider Role (HEPR) not inherent or inevitable, but that it has many negative consequences for industrialized societies, for their political, economic, family and heterosexual social systems, as well as for the individual and its sociopolitical participation." [184] Grønseth and others press their point too far when they contend that current marital structure is responsible for many of society's

179. Ford, p. 42.
180. Mead, 1967, p. 873.
181. D'Andrade, p. 201.
182. *Ibid.*
183. *Ibid.*
184. Grønseth, p. 1.

ills.[185] Present family patterns cannot, as some suggest, be blamed for poverty, crime, mental illness, alienation, even war, anymore than problems in the larger black community can be blamed on weaknesses in the black family—a gross error in which some scholars allowed themselves to be trapped some years ago.

Nevertheless, the arguments of Scandinavian researchers such as Grønseth, Holter, and Dahlberg among others, that the present pattern of "husband as unique provider" gives rise to many strains and tensions both in and out of the family, helps us to call further into question (alongside D'Andrade's findings) the inevitability of the inequality that Ford asserts is born out of inherent maleness and femaleness. Holter notes, for instance, the large body of research showing that women generally have lower levels of self-esteem than men, and more often than men they possess feelings of worthlessness. "Being an adult woman in an instrumentally oriented society may contribute to self-devaluation because the female role makes it impossible for women to realize their goals. The fact that many women can experience success only vicariously, through identification with their husbands, does not provide sufficient fulfillment for the more talented. The opportunities that women have to attain high social prestige and wealth by marriage without striving for it in a 'proper' way may corrode rather than enhance their self-respect." [186] Her point simply is that since part of the essence of any modern society (whether capitalist, socialist, or communist) is achievement, female passivity can be an unrewarding and even punishing posture to maintain. Since achievement is ideologically and theoretically open to all, it follows that some women will reject passivity, seek the rewards of achievement, and gain equality of status and power with men.

Rapidity and Extensiveness of Change

Therefore, the real question is not, "Can women be equal with men"; or "Is the model of marriage in Figure 5.1 actually feasible?" It would appear that the answer is "yes" on both counts, so that the more pertinent issue is, "How many persons will actually be affected by such a model?" A recent study of American women college students reaffirmed what earlier studies had shown—not more than 20 percent of these women aspired to achievement-oriented careers.[187] Rossi, in a study of 15,000 women college graduates all around age twenty-five, found that the percentage of them pursuing traditional, feminine domestic roles actually *increased* in the three years between college graduation and the

185. Otto, pp. 51, 52, 185–86, 189.
186. Holter, pp. 243–44.
187. Walshok, pp. 40ff.

time of her survey.[188] There are other studies which likewise suggest that women, in America and Europe, once they finish school, and in spite of strong career aspirations they might have had while there, tend to relax their career dedication substantially.[189]

It may be especially difficult for lower-class black women, who for so long have been *forced* into the sole-provider role and have had no choice but to take menial and low-paying jobs, to absorb the notion that the role of coprovider is a privilege to be sought after. The same may be said of white women who have been unwillingly forced into the role of sole provider by reason of husband illness, unemployment, or his simple refusal to work. However, these are not conditions of genuine role-interchangeability as described above, but instead situations of role-reversal in which women have, against their will, lost the option *not* to work.

Another common situation of role-reversal, but one which the wife generally takes on voluntarily, has occurred while the husband is in school and the wife provides for him and any children. There is no evidence, however, that up to this time, either sex has regarded this kind of arrangement as ideal or other than expedient. It seems to be perceived as pragmatic and temporary, and most often, as soon as the husband is able to provide, plans are made for the wife to drop out of the labor force, to stay home and care for any children present, or to have another child.

We should also remember that women from blue-collar homes (whether white or black) have been severely underrepresented among the ranks of Feminists, who have been largely middle-class. Whatever the gradual rate at which middle-class women come to adopt "modern" definitions of their own roles, the rate among working-class women will probably be substantially less. It would seem to take more incentive than a job on an assembly line or in a variety store to motivate moderately educated women to press seriously for new marital arrangements. It is those well-educated women with career opportunities who will initially have the desire and ability to bargain and challenge for new patterns.

Furthermore, we cannot overlook the opposition of men, the ruling status group, to changes of this magnitude. "It is reasonable," argues Holter, "to expect women to be more dissatisfied than men with present sex role norms . . . [because] men have more power and prestige than women." [190] From studies in Norway, Holter presents data which verifies the expectation that men more than women are likely to favor the conjugal status quo. Men and women were compared on their responses

188. Rossi, 1970, p. 6.
189. Turner, p. 279; Figes, pp. 169–70.
190. Holter, pp. 90–91, 230.

to a series of questions on traditional vs. nontraditional attitudes and behaviors for women ("men should leave domestic work to women"; "women ought to get as many chances for advancement in occupational life as men"; and so forth).[191] She found that 32 percent of the men but only 11 percent of the women were classified as *most traditional*. Conversely, 41 percent of the women and only 15 percent of the men were *least* traditional, while 48 percent of the women and 53 percent of the men were *intermediate* in their responses.[192] She also shows comparisons on "norms concerning the division of work between men and women," and finds that 24 percent of the women and only 7 percent of the men "prefer a new division of work in the family and in occupational life"; 43 percent of the women and 42 percent of the men "think women should combine domestic and occupational work"; and only 28 percent of the women compared to 49 percent (half) of the men "prefer women to be mothers and housewives." [193]

While there is not yet much American data available that is directly comparable with Holter's Scandinavian data on male resistance to this fundamental change, there is some information which indicates that the same kind of male opposition does indeed exist in the United States. Kaley, for instance, found clear evidence that "while the married professional women had positive attitudes toward the professional woman's dual role [career and marriage], the married professional men . . . had negative attitudes. The investigator concluded that negative attitudes toward the professional woman's dual role . . . are an indication of why few women prepare themselves for and pursue professional careers." [194]

Steinmann and her associates have used questions that describe behaviors in which the woman sees her own satisfactions coming second after husband and children and family responsibilities ahead of any potential occupational activity.[195] A sample item: "I prefer to listen rather than to talk." Other items they used delineated a self-oriented woman who considers her own satisfactions equally important with those of husband and family, and who wishes to have opportunities to realize any latent ability or talent. For example: "It's unfair that married women have to compromise their ideals." The results of administering both kinds of items to samples of men and women (mostly white) consistently reveal the following patterns: females tend to see themselves as actually holding both the traditional and modern orientations in

---

191. *Ibid.*, p. 57.
192. *Ibid.*, p. 70.
193. *Ibid.*, p. 71.
194. Kaley, p. 305.
195. Steinmann, et al., 1968.

somewhat of a balance, and they perceive this kind of balance to be ideal. Yet when females respond to how they think *men* want them to behave, they report that men want them to be more oriented toward the family than toward self-actualization.

Men, when asked about their definitions of the female sex role, tend to respond in equalitarian fashion. They say that women should hold both traditional and modern behaviors in balance. Therefore, on the one side, there is *verbally* stated agreement between females and males on how women *should* behave, but on the other, women *do not believe* that men actually hold a balanced view with respect to female behavior. One could interpret this dissensus as do the investigators, i.e., "reflecting lack of communication between the sexes as to the kind of women actually desired by men." [196] The implication they draw is that what is needed is "the establishment of programs bringing together . . . husbands and wives, in candid . . . discussion of . . . expectations in the area of sex-role behavior." [197] This interpretation assumes that if husbands and wives only *knew* that they basically agree on how a wife should behave, then she would be freer to move in that direction.

But if one thinks of males and females as competing interest groups, then the interpretation is not quite so simple. One might agree with Goode that men are far more willing to grant equality on the ideological and verbal levels than they are on the actual behavior levels.[198] Hence, the findings reported above may simply reflect a verbal statement from the male standpoint. In reality, they may not want their own wives to behave in self-oriented fashion because, inevitably, this means certain costs on their part. Likewise, women may in fact be accurately representing how men *behave* when they (females) contend that males prefer a family-oriented woman.

When Steinmann and her associates investigated *male* sex-role definitions, they once again unearthed divergence. Men believed themselves to be rather balanced between the performance of family and self-oriented (occupational) roles.[199] Women, however, perceived that men were exceedingly more occupation-oriented than they were family oriented. In short, women see men making the occupational world their primary concern, the family a subordinate concern, and wanting women to content themselves primarily with this subordinate role. Men see women trying to pull them into still greater involvement with family concerns than they already maintain or consider justified.

196. *Ibid.*
197. *Ibid.*
198. Goode, 1963, pp. 54ff.
199. Steinmann, et al.

What is particularly intriguing is that many women evidently prefer to pull men into a similar type of role-balance that they seek for themselves. Evidently, it is not that most women wish to forsake traditional roles; instead, they apparently seek to balance them with modern roles. But in order to do this effectively, they believe that males must add to their occupational roles certain traditional familial ones as well. And in spite of what men *say*, it is not at all clear that many American men have been or are yet prepared to behave in this fashion. The items used in the Steinmann studies are attitudinal, and there is no available behavioral evidence that American men, any more than Scandinavian men, are shifting in any significant numbers in this direction. Instead, as Rossi suggests, most men seem to prefer current

> sex [role] differentiation [which] is functional to the perpetuation of a male-dominated society in which the family system is the shock-absorbing handmaiden of the occupational system. The "unmanly" ridicule directed to men who play a significant role in the care of their children, or the "unfeminine" charge directed at women who dislike home duties and seek to participate in the occupational system with a style comparable to that of men, both serve the function of supporting a social system in which aggressive high-need achievement men are free to devote most of their energies to the occupational system while women are taught to seek their major gratifications by vicariously living through their men and their children.[200]

Nevertheless, in spite of the fact that as yet there is little hard data on any current *widespread* female class consciousness as described by Oppenheimer that might lead to conflict and significant role-changes overnight, there are at the same time increasing bits of evidence that a growing minority (Jessie Bernard estimates 10 to 15 percent)[201] of women (most of whom are not "kooks" or extremists) have a genuine career commitment that would necessarily modify marital arrangements in the direction of Figure 5.1.[202] Furthermore, according to Rossi, we are likely to witness increasing numbers of women in their thirties being dissatisfied with the traditional behaviors they have carried out for years and beginning to adopt genuinely "modern" role-behaviors.[203] It is not that they will go to work merely for money or to escape boredom, as so many women in that age bracket already do. Instead, their behaviors will reflect strong desires for achievement and contain genuine career

200. Rossi, 1970.
201. Bernard, 1970, *The Futurist*.
202. Bird, p. 184; Rossi, 1969, 1970.
203. *Ibid.*, 1970.

commitment and determination along the lines manifested by our hypothetical Mrs. French.

When it comes to long-range alterations in sex-role definitions, neo-Feminists have scrutinized the kind of education that children receive in our school systems.[204] As indicated in chapter three, the learning of "maleness" by boys and "femaleness" by girls begins early in nursery school. According to Horner, schools contribute a great deal toward the learning by most women of a psychological *need to avoid success,* especially when competing with male students.[205] As long as the learning process communicates that women be passive and prepare for feminine roles in life, many of them are likely to come to adulthood with traditional role-definitions. Changes in curriculum and in other school matters that stress sex equality are as difficult to institute as school changes that remove racial stereotypes and promote race equality. Unlike Sweden and the USSR, where the national government controls the local schools and is establishing policies aimed at achieving sex equality, the American federal government does not control local schools, nor are few if any local governments committed to any such policy.

In view of the American recession of 1969–71 and the unemployment of large numbers of men, what are the prospects for sufficient numbers of occupations and careers for both women *and* men to enter? Oppenheimer bases her projections on continued economic expansion. Certainly, if increasing numbers of women become career oriented, then the supply of jobs must expand correspondingly.[206] Some economists point to certain nonconsumer areas in American society that could have great future growth potential: law, corrections, medicine, agencies for saving our cities including those concerned with problems of transportation, housing, pollution, and so forth.[207] This says nothing, of course, about the growth of consumer-oriented and service industries not only in the United States, but particularly in Europe (East and West) where the demand for consumer goods in most countries still outstrips the supply. And what of the Third World: Latin America, Africa, China, the Middle and Far East?

Virtually every developing nation has a commitment to modernization, though some are ideologically frigid toward either capitalism or communism. As these vast sections of the world modernize, job opportunities will be created, and Americans and Europeans may be allowed to compete with nationals for these jobs. Therefore, instead of having to move from Iowa to New York to take a job, one may have to be

---

204. *See* Morgan, 1970, pp. 360ff.; Rossi, 1970.
205. Horner, 1970.
206. *See* Bird, chapter 10.
207. Berger and Berger, *The New Republic.*

willing to move to any spot in the world. Indeed, nationals from numerous countries may be competing with a variety of other nationals for positions that may be available at any time, anywhere in the world. This worldwide, geographic mobility may place an even greater strain on marriages where both spouses are career oriented. A husband working in New York while his wife works in Washington is one thing; but one spouse working in London and the other in Tokyo is quite another.

We noted above that in the Soviet Union and Sweden extensive daycare facilities are one means to relieve parents of the responsibilities of child care so that both are free to work. In the United States there are few such quality facilities and most working women use *ad hoc* means of care such as hiring a neighbor or friend to watch the kids.[208] Though there has been some discussion at the federal and state levels about constructing facilities for women who are currently on welfare so that they can work, little action has yet been taken. And to construct such facilities for middle-class women who want to work primarily for purposes of achievement is a concept foreign to most politicians and many citizens.

Hence, in the immediate future, we should not expect the United States to have anywhere near the child-care facilities that certain other nations have. Many American parents are quite reluctant to entrust the rearing of their children to "outsiders." Some feel it might harm the child to be deprived of the unique love that its own mother is believed to have for it. Others feel that their children might be exposed to "alien" values and ideas. One solution in a marriage where the wife is achievement oriented lies "in a greater participation in the supervision and care of children on the husband's part." Even in Sweden, however, where this is the professed ideal, it is difficult to get husbands to cut back on their own occupational activities and to share more in child care, as it is in Russia and certainly in the United States.[209]

Therefore, if day-care facilities are not available or deemed desirable, and if husbands generally refuse to share more of the duties of child care, then achievement-oriented women will probably decide to have fewer children. It is already the case that women who work in Europe and in the U.S. have fewer children than women who do not work.[210] It could very well be that in the years ahead not only will more achievement-oriented women remain single, but more of those who do marry will choose to have no children at all; and among those who want children, the great majority may opt for one or two.

An acid test of a woman's commitment to modernity is her preference

208. Ruderman, Part IV.
209. Sandlund, p. 5.
210. *See* Scanzoni, 1971. The cause and effect sequence is not totally clear.

for occupational rewards rather than more children, and such preferences are strongly correlated with the model of marriage structure in Figure 5.1. There is also already some evidence that mothers who define their roles in more modern terms tend to have fewer children than mothers who define themselves in traditional terms.[211] Farley, moreover, found that women graduate students who are career oriented desired fewer children than students who were not career oriented.[212]

Case Studies in Role-Interchangeability

Systematic survey data on marriages in which role-interchangeability and equality of power and status exist are virtually impossible to obtain, since these few marriages are so widely scattered. However, we can draw on case studies to answer two related questions. First, in the gradual transition from role-specialization to interchangeability, what kinds of occupations lend themselves most readily to the new patterns? Second, what specific bits of information can help us better understand the dynamics of this very different kind of marital structure?

In the evolution of these new patterns, occupations in which one or both partners have maximum flexibility to plan their own work schedules will very likely be the first ones to attract achievement-oriented women stably married to sympathetic males. For example, we would not expect to find for some time to come middle- or top-level business executives married to each other. There are just too many immediate and unforeseen demands placed on such persons to allow the kind of flexibility that women especially need to be ultimately responsible for household and child-rearing duties. During this transitional stage and perhaps for some time, household duties will, in the final analysis, remain *ultimately* the province even of achievement-oriented of wives (though they may not perform the duties themselves but hire household help and outside care for children when they are young).

However, regardless of the husband's occupation, a wife who has a skill she can perform at home maximizes her flexibility and avoids basic conflict. She may be an artist, free-lance writer, music teacher, composer, and so forth. One account shows that this kind of pattern can work equally well the other way—the wife is an art director for an ad agency and commutes daily to Stockholm, while the husband stays at home, practices free-lance writing, does the housework, and cares for the child.[213] In an analogous situation, the husband is an artist and paints at his home studio and takes care of the children, while the wife teaches Ger-

211. Clarkson, et al.
212. Farley.
213. Durham, p. 46.

man at the college level.[214] During her graduate training he worked as a janitor to supplement her fellowship.

In another actual situation, the husband is a stockbroker for a large firm that has offices all over the United States. His wife is a professor of physical therapy in a university. If she decided to move to another university, he would be able to move with her to most places because his firm would automatically allow him to transfer to their branch in that new locale. If there were no branch, he could very easily obtain a position with another brokerage firm, since his income depends largely on commissions. Many types of experienced salesmen have this geographic flexibility. If, on the other hand, his firm wanted to transfer him where there was no university in which his wife could or would want to teach, he would turn down the transfer.[215] Thus for the sake of her achievement, he would limit his. At the same time, for her side of the bargain, and since college professors have considerable control over their work schedules, his wife is able to be chiefly responsible for the care of their eight-year-old son.

College teaching is, of course, a prime example where both partners can hold the same kind of job, be coachievers, and yet minimize the likelihood of basic conflict. Time schedules can be adjusted so that one partner is home caring for the children (yet grading papers or preparing for the next class) while the other is actually in class, or in committee, and vice-versa. Moreover, it is the kind of occupation that readily lends itself to the goal of some Feminists for "twenty-hour jobs." That is, some Feminists would prefer situations in which *each* partner works twenty hours per week, rather than having both work forty hours or more. By this means, they argue, neither partner gets "overinvolved" in the occupation, and they have more time for each other and the children. A twenty-hour job would also permit highly trained young women to keep up with their fields if they chose not to work full-time while a child is still small. A microbiologist, for example, cannot afford to withdraw from her field for even one year or she would be hopelessly out-of-touch. Universities and colleges can make twenty-hour appointments to teach reduced loads or to engage part-time in a research project.

Jessie Bernard notes that, in fact, singleness is the lot of the great majority of academic women and attributes this to factors such as a monastic tradition, a vocation for celibacy, and lack of peer support.[216] Up to this time, dedicated women scholars have found singleness more compatible with university demands than being married. Some academic women are married, of course, but Bernard reports that among most of

---

214. Bloomington, Indiana, *Herald-Telephone* (May 20, 1971).
215. Personal conversation.
216. Bernard, *Academic Women*, pp. 206ff.

those she studied (up to around 1960) the work role seemed to remain secondary to the wife-mother role.[217] Nevertheless, she presents three case studies of what she calls "the wave of the future," in which each person, in each marriage, is a scholar and is attached to a university. One couple consists of two biologists who, before the birth of the first child, spent fifteen hours a day, six or seven days a week, working together on the same experiments.[218] We might expect that equal access to external resources resulted in equal partner-status within their marriage. However, the advent of children limited the wife's hours in the lab since she, not the husband, took prime responsibility for child care. Yet she maintains several hours a day in the lab, and as the children go to school she expects to increase her lab work. It seems clear that as the children grow older, and she is able once again to gain resources at a par with her husband, she will be equal to him in marital power and status. Note, however, that as far as we know, she does not choose to bargain or conflict with him for equality while the children are young—she does not insist that he be quite as responsible as she for child care. Thus at that stage she is dependent on him and fulfills more of a junior-partner status.

A second couple is basically similar except that while they are both political scientists, they have different subspecializations; hence, they do not always work together as closely as the biologists. In the third case, each spouse is in a totally different field though with some minimum overlap (economics and history). All three cases represent the transitional stage through which most Western societies seem to be passing as they gradually move from role-specialization to the not yet totally clear outlines of role-interchangeability. During this era, achievement-oriented women are asserting their rights for individual attainments, but in most instances, they have not been able, or willing, to bargain or conflict with men fully enough to get them to cut back on their own achievements and assume equal responsibility for child care.

Achievement-oriented women married to higher-status men, unlike our Mrs. French, have not up to now (except for those in the entertainment industry) been so ready to bargain with the ultimate threat of divorce if their husbands are reluctant to concede certain privileges. The overall reward-cost ratio, for reasons discussed earlier, is after all quite favorable to them. Therefore, to avoid basic conflict and possible dissolution, one respondent told Bernard:

> I wouldn't advise any woman to combine a scientific research career with marriage unless she had a husband who thoroughly understood the special demands of that career, was in sympathy with them, and wanted his wife

217. *Ibid.*, p. 215.
218. *Ibid.*, pp. 231ff.

to pursue them. To be successful at both marriage and career a woman must "choose" her mate carefully.[219]

Bernard assumed that the determination of a wife's career lies not with herself but with her husband, and that if she is to avoid basic conflict and divorce, she must obtain the consent, approval, and support of her husband before she pursues her career.[220] Significantly, the assumption that a career woman's self-determination is limited compared to her husband's is considerably different from the one underlying a later statement in which Bernard acknowledges that the whole thrust of Feminism is to achieve equality of self-determination; and that if a married woman cannot have this freedom there is no fixed or inherent reason that she should not seek divorce.[221]

The broad question of the feasibility of the twenty-hour week, espoused by some Feminists, is a thorny one, and critics point out that career-oriented professional and business persons simply cannot, and most often would not, turn their achievement endeavors off and on like a water faucet. Whether in government, law, business, or education, the committed person is *constantly* coping with a host of immediate responsibilities, or else planning for the numerous ones next in line. Recall Wilensky's data earlier in the chapter showing that such persons tend to work fifty-five hours per week or more. As far as achievement-oriented men are concerned, it is not likely that in the future many of them will even consider cutting back to a twenty-hour work week. Just how many achievement-oriented women would want or be able to obtain twenty-hour positions in the future is not clear at this time.

A particularly significant case-study of what appears to be a genuine case of marital role-interchangeability is found in Mrs. Patricia Roberts Harris, a black woman and a lawyer in a prominent Washington firm, who was appointed in 1965 to be Ambassador to Luxembourg.[222] She also serves on the board of directors of I.B.M. When she first went to Luxembourg, her husband (they are middle-aged and childless), also a lawyer, gave up his Washington practice to accompany her. Her own comments about female role-definitions give us some clue as to her own achievement orientation:

> I hate to hear people say a woman is charming. I don't want to be loved. I want to be esteemed.

The fact that she possesses more prestige and power (and perhaps income) than her husband does not seem to threaten him: "Nothing surpasses be-

219. *Ibid.*, pp. 220, 237.
220. *Ibid.*, p. 231.
221. Bernard, 1970, *The Futurist.*
222. *See* Yette.

ing married to a really intelligent woman," he says. "They always know how to treat their men." It would appear that each person in that marriage sees himself and his spouse as coprovider: equal in responsibility and privilege, therefore equal in power and status.

The few case studies we have been able to gather obviously do not exhaust all the instances of equal-partner marriage in the United States or elsewhere. There are surely others (probably more outside than inside the U.S.), and in the future it is virtually certain there will be an ever-increasing number of them. Furthermore, for reasons suggested earlier, the proportion may increase more rapidly in black than in white society.

PROSPECTS FOR MONOGAMOUS MARRIAGE

There is one final issue to be considered and that is: in view of a model like Figure 5.1, which speaks to the Feminist goal of self-determination and economic independence for women, and in view of the decline in the numbers and importance of children, why marry at all? If women can be independent achievers and gain those kinds of gratifications and rewards on their own, if both sexes can obtain hetero- and homosexual gratifications at will, if friendships can be established (with either sex apart from marriage) to fulfill cognitive and psychoemotional needs, and if children necessary to replace society can be produced whenever required and then placed in state homes, why would one man and one woman ever want to enter into monogamous marriage?

There is obviously no unambiguous answer to this question. Even those who indicate that the foreseeable future will evolve many different varieties of family experimentation freely acknowledge that for the overwhelming majority of people in modern society, monogamous marriage will be the preferred pattern.[223] They also acknowledge that a goodly number of these persons will be bound together by the *interdependence* described in Figure 4.1. As we saw, this interdependence is based on an *exchange* of rewards and benefits between unequals. People enter contemporary marriage with its role-specialization because they believe they can obtain rewards there that they can obtain in no comparable setting. It is safe to say that in the foreseeable future an increasing number of people will enter monogamous marriages based on *role-interchangeability* for the same reason—it is *perceived by them* to be a *unique reward-producing* center.

We pointed out in Figure 5.1 how exchanges between *equal* partners could contribute to reward satisfactions, and thus to stability, in ways

223. Otto, *passim.*

that are similar to, and perhaps even more significant than, exchanges between unequals. We shall now elaborate on that point as well as on the broader issue of why the great bulk of persons keep gravitating toward conjugal marriage—whether based on specialization or interchangeability. Three of the four following factors, in combination, form a cluster of rewards that seem to draw persons in modern society to this form of marriage.[224] If in the distant future, marriage ceases, for whatever reason, to provide one or more of these rewards, or some other social structure could supply them more adequately, then marriage as we know it might very well totally cease to exist.

INEFFICACY OF THE KIN

This first factor is not a reward in the same sense as the other three. Instead, as a preface to these three factors, the point must be reiterated that with the advent of industrialization the kin loses its hold over the husband-wife unit. As Ariés puts it—the line gives way to the family. This decline occurs, in large measure, because the line no longer has the economic and political resources to maintain control of the nuclear unit. The husband-wife unit looks, instead, to political, educational, and economic formal organizations for resources and rewards.

Nevertheless there are processes of exchange maintained between kin even in modern society.[225] A middle-aged couple may help finance a younger married son or daughter through college in exchange for visits, affection, and even influence over certain decisions affecting the younger couple. But ultimately, since the impersonal occupational structure can supply greater rewards (nontangible and tangible) than the kin, it tends to exercise greater control over the behavior of the young couple. In particular, the couple must be prepared for geographic and perhaps social mobility. Though the kin might prefer to have the couple nearby, the couple might, in response to occupational demands, have to move a great distance away. And if the couple become part of a social class that is higher than that of their kin, the *social distance* between them may, in many respects, become unbridgeable.

We looked earlier at proposals that the family of the future be based on nonblood kinlike ties. Whether or not such kin ties will emerge depends on whether they can offer any rewards to the husband-wife unit that are not now being supplied to it, or cannot be gotten elsewhere. Clearly, the tribe cannot offer the same achievement rewards that organizations, professions, and businesses within modern societies offer. Like-

224. The following discussion, in part, is drawn from Scanzoni, 1971, pp. 311ff.
225. Sussman, 1966.

wise, commitment to a tribe (blood or nonblood) restricts geographic mobility demands which, as noted above, may become increasingly world-wide in scope.[226]

The commune represents an effort to resuscitate the tribal concept, and many of its members have indeed rejected achievement orientations. But it does not yet appear likely that the majority of the world's citizens (especially women) are prepared to reject modern society and live in a kibbutzlike setting. Until and unless such wholesale repudiation occurs, there is little, in the minds of most persons, that a return to the tribe has to offer; hence, it does not appear that the tribe will swallow up the conjugal pattern anytime soon. At the most, we might very well expect to see more of Stoller's "intimate networks," because these do provide valuable emotional resources to the husband-wife unit; but as we saw, they in no way blur distinctive family boundaries nor the autonomy of these units.

THE ECONOMIC-STATUS DIMENSION

Assuming that in the foreseeable future most persons will accept the achievement ethos, why should they marry if women can earn economic and status benefits on their own? One obvious answer is the pooling of resources that can result. At present the social status of husband *and* wife is assessed almost always on the basis of the husband's occupation, even if the wife works, usually because her income tends to be much lower than his. But when the notion of career oriented wives becomes more institutionalized, and wives' earning power approximates that of their husbands, an accurate measure of family status will not be possible unless the wife's occupation is taken into account along with the husband's. Two fairly high incomes can produce a life style obviously more affluent than one.

Husband-wife, or conjugal, marriage has been, and evidently will continue to remain, a kind of structural *center* for the display of consumption symbols that accord social status to them by the community, and thus a sense of personal worth to husband, wife, and any offspring.[227] Given the stress, especially in America, on visible success, some such center or focal point is virtually requisite. Conversely, in most kibbutzim where the emphasis on individual occupational achievements is relatively muted, there is less need for *consumption centers*.

But even if some career-oriented men could accept the notion that wives have an equal right to occupational achievement, that it is a good thing for their wives' income to substantially boost the family life style,

226. *See* Scanzoni, 1971, pp. 135–36.
227. *Ibid.*, p. 320.

and that they have as much right to be supported by wives as vice-versa, still these three things by themselves might be insufficient inducements to get men into, or once there to remain in, situations of role-interchangeability.

There is, however, an additional inducement or reward in equal-partner situations that might be particularly compelling to career-oriented men, as well as to such women. "Specialization," says Blau, "provides each man with more of some resources than he can use and fewer of others than he needs. It therefore necessitates exchanges. 'Exchange without specialization is impossible; specialization without exchange is silly.' " [228] Does this imply that when husbands and wives are equal in resources, they therefore have nothing to exchange at the instrumental level, nothing to gain from entering into or maintaining a marriage relationship? If one person earns $25,000 per year, would an equal amount earned by the other simply be merely a matter of what the economists call "marginal utility," that is, one's income is already at such a level that additional increments really do not boost family life style all that much? Perhaps, but probably not, given a society where there seems to be no ceiling on consumption aspirations.

But whatever the answer to that question, "advice exchanged in mutual partnerships . . . between individuals whose competence is about the same . . . [can be mutually profitable] because the advice two colleagues exchange tends to be superior to their decisions on their own cases. . . . each partner preferring the less anxiety-distorted decisions of the other to his own, permits both to benefit from their mutual exchange of advice." [229]

Blau's idea is illustrated in Bernard's case studies. A husband (research scientist) describes what happened as his wife "emerged into professional competence" as teacher and researcher:

A new partnership feeling developed. My pride in her achievements matched hers in mine. Slowly and hesitantly we became able to discuss serious questions with serious regard for one another's opinions.[230]

Another wife described how she and her husband would discuss critiques of the research papers and books that the other had written. And while this was sometimes "painful," she said, "it has benefited our [marital] relationship immeasurably." [231] In other words, husbands and wives who are equally involved in a career may be able to exchange certain benefits that are unknown in role-specialized marriages. These benefits consist of

228. Blau, p. 170.
229. *Ibid.*, pp. 170–71.
230. Bernard, 1964, *Academic Women*, p. 218.
231. *Ibid.*, p. 240.

the exchange of colleague advice, criticism, suggestions, counsel, and so on, that occur between persons who are equally involved in career patterns. Such exchange does not require them to be involved in exactly the same occupation or organization. It does not mean a revival of the "mama-papa" small business, which is obviously a thing of the past. But in a very real sense, it does imply the same kind of interdependence for, as Figes notes, husbands and wives operating a small business together with domestic quarters on the premises were certainly bound together in a very strong way.[232]

Under current patterns of role-specialization, the wife can "comfort, understand, sympathize with, and generally encourage" her husband in his career activities, but in many cases there is a limit to her empathy.[233] And, in exchange, she often expects him to empathize with her in her routine household and child-care activities which may seem dull and boring to him in comparison to what he thinks are his much more interesting occupational activities. Although it varies by social class, many husbands feel that wives are not interested in their world of work; or if they are, they do not understand it because they are not obliged to "work like a man," or else they do not understand because their work behaviors are too esoteric for women, whose whole life focuses on activities so radically different from theirs.[234]

If, however, each were involved in careers, each might perceive a valuable sounding board in the other. As in Bernard's cases, each may be able to feel that the other can actually "take my role," "understand," "put himself in my position," and that "I can do the same for him," in ways that are perhaps more meaningful than are now possible. Therefore, permanent, ongoing exchanges within marriage between genuine equals, focusing on mutual advice and counsel pertinent to career behaviors and decisions, may be extremely rewarding to both partners and thus provide the motivation to enter and maintain such a relationship.

EXPRESSIVE GRATIFICATIONS

While the media have given much publicity to the so-called "sexual revolution," there is no evidence up to this time of any widespread sexual promiscuity in American society. Even among those who violate certain taboos, such as nudists or swingers, strong norms prevail to ritualize their behaviors. Most significant, as we saw, is the growing awareness of many Feminists that freer sex is not correlated with sex equality, and the con-

---

232. Figes, pp. 69–70.
233. Scanzoni, 1970, chapter 4.
234. *Ibid.;* Komarovsky, 1962.

tention by some of them that celibacy or lesbianism might be preferable to what they consider heterosexual exploitation.

In any case, Figure 5.1 assumes that in the foreseeable future most persons in our society will continue to look to a monogamous marital relationship for their major fulfillment, not only for sexual gratification, but also for companionship and empathy. As there has always been, there will always be "deviation" sexually, both pre- and extramaritally. At the same time, if more women become determined to avoid sexual exploitation, they could possibly have a braking effect on the trend toward greater sexual permissiveness, or at least keep the trend from accelerating beyond its present pace. Moreover, given the range and depth of the exchanges in marriages based on interchangeability, there is reason to believe that marital expressive gratifications (including sex) may, in the future, become more rewarding to greater numbers of people.

For instance, we have just seen that one dimension of empathy may actually be enhanced when partners are coachievers. And thinking back to our earlier comparison of Figures 4.1 and 5.1, we saw that under role-specialization merely one partner, the husband, exchanges economic-status rewards for the wife's expressive rectitudes, whereas under interchangeability *both* partners are *simultaneously* exchanging economic-status rewards for the expressive rectitudes of the other. These simultaneous mutual interchanges may have a cumulative effect on the positive evaluation of these benefits. In the future, therefore, as more women become achievement oriented and desirous of egalitarianism, they may: (1) be more motivated to avoid exploitative sex than at present; (2) seek for equal-partnership marriages (or else remain single); (3) find these new marital arrangements (as may men) more rewarding expressively (as well as economically) than is presently so in many instances.

GRATIFICATION THROUGH CHILDREN

Hoffman and Wyatt have observed that up to now most women receive a sense of identity, creativity, and achievement through motherhood.[235] But besides a woman's *reason for being*, and besides the expressive gratification and enjoyment children bring to mothers and fathers, children also supply another reward to both parents:

. . . in a modern, achievement-oriented society, children and their attainments are viewed . . . as rewards. . . . the achievements of the children reflect back on the parents and provide . . . prestige and status for them. Children . . . become another status symbol in a society whose status order rests on the display of just such symbols. . . . it is in the interest of par-

235. Hoffman and Wyatt, 1960.

ents to aid their children. . . . The more "successful" or at least "respectable" their child is, the greater the degree of reward and gratification this provides to parents.[236]

Although in the past children have, for several reasons, been one important incentive to marry, will they lose their significance as a reward factor in the future? Will this be especially so in those marriages where the wife is coachiever with her husband? Probably so in quantitative terms, for there is already some evidence that women who define themselves in more modern terms tend to have fewer children than those who do not. When, during the years ahead, equals are exchanging economic-status and expressive rewards in the manner we have been describing, neither partner will probably have as great a need for as many children as now. Equally critical is the restriction of children on the flexibility to pursue a career.

At the same time, we must not lose sight of the highly important reward of the child as status symbol to parents, through his or her achievements. Even in some kibbutzim, where individual achievement for parent and child alike has supposedly been rendered meaningless through collective ownership of goods and property, and where parents have relatively little influence on the child's future aspirations because of collective child-rearing, there is still evidence that certain parents maintain close ties with their children, and actually try to provide them with additional consumer goods.[237] Whether consciously willed or not, certain differences and inequalities are generated among some kibbutz children, differences that tend to gratify the parents: "Look at how well off my child is compared to others through what I have been able to do for him."[238]

Similarly, in the Soviet Union, in spite of a great push toward extended day-care facilities and boarding schools, there is great concern that parents and children maintain close ties. In fact, one of the strong selling points to Soviet parents for these facilities is that their children will be so much better prepared for future achievement opportunities than would otherwise be possible.[239] Hence, what in a communist country appears to prevent children and their achievements from being sources of gratification to parents in reality turns out to enhance that very bonding process. Moreover, given that achievement orientations will not diminish in future industrial societies, and that more and more women will personally come to internalize them, there is no reason to believe that parents will not continue to consider (perhaps unconsciously) the child they have as a potential added source of gratification through his-her achievements.

236. Scanzoni, 1971, p. 318.
237. Shepher, pp. 567ff.
238. Scanzoni, 1971, p. 318.
239. Bronfenbrenner, p. 112.

But a radical departure from the present may very well be that *one* child of *either* sex will suffice for this kind of reward. Presently, if a couple has one child, or two (or more) of the same sex, it is common for them to reason that they ought to try just once more to see if they can get one of the opposite sex, especially a boy who is more likely than a girl to "attain" in such things as athletics or occupation. Presumably among coachiever marriages, the sex of the first (perhaps only) child will have no influence on parental aspirations for it. Since the parents themselves hold to career orientations for both sexes, they will almost certainly socialize their child similarly. Irrespective of its sex, therefore, they can expect that it too will become achievement oriented, and supply to them a much sought-after reward in modern society.

To sum up these factors regarding monogamous marriage we may say: (1) that unless and until large numbers of modern persons reject achievement values, it is difficult to see how tribal experiments can come to replace, except for a few persons, the clearly identifiable and autonomous husband-wife unit; (2) that these autonomous units have persisted because they have been a source of economic and status gratifications, and under conditions of genuine equality may supply still additional socioeconomic and novel colleague rewards; (3) that likewise, as these units have in the past supplied certain levels of expressive rewards, interchangeability could conceivably generate even greater levels of these rewards (including sexual); (4) that many dual-achiever units will continue to produce at least one child, maintain close and unique ties with it, and seek the dual gratifications that a child can supply to parents in modern society.

CONCLUSION

The future of marriage is indeed an unsettled matter. One way to assess these uncertainties is to assume, as we have, that marriage will continue to be a long-term, ongoing confrontation between the sexes that is inexorably moving toward role-equality. There are important variations on this theme—communal living, and so forth—but so far few if any of them have been able to demonstrate or to maintain sex equality. The key to equality is not "the abolishment of the family," but access by women to those resources which will enable them to bargain and conflict for equality. In modern societies, whether capitalist, socialist, or communist, this means self-determination and freedom for women to achieve within the occupational sector on the same basis as any other *person,* irrespective of *sex* or *color.*

Achievement-oriented women must necessarily change the structure of marriage from its basis of role-specialization to role-interchangeability, *ergo* equality. But self-determination and freedom have never yet come about without social conflict, nor at the human level, without considerable pain and suffering. Marital tensions and divorces may very well rise before (if ever) they abate. Men will not easily give up their rights, privileges, and power within the occupational and domestic spheres. Only as women choose to press the conflict both at the group and individual levels will change eventually come about.

Perhaps the following comments by Max Lerner summarize in as sober, succinct, and responsible a fashion as possible just what the situation is now, and what trends toward the foreseeable future seem to be emerging:

> . . . the American college girl [is] thoughtful, alert, independent, and cool toward the zanier aspects of Women's Lib. Yet . . . her imagination has been caught by what the women writers and organizers have been saying. . . . things never will be the same again in women's minds and between women and men. The life choices they face are bound to be different than those of their mothers a couple of decades earlier. Everything then came wrapped up in a single package . . . labeled "marriage and family" and while in some cases there were preliminary explorations of sex and a job in a big city before marriage, there never was any question that these were marginal and never any question of what the goal and core of life were. *What is happening* now is . . . that the world is opening up for them as never before. It is the rare girl today who doesn't want to find some work that is hers, that she can pursue through her life, as men have done for centuries. . . . The girls haven't yet been completely sold but they are listening as never before. . . . But with the chance of freedom come also the choices, ambiguities, confusions, burdens as never before. Many women may not have the strength to face the new freedoms and the new choices. But if they do, I suspect that their daughters will be happy they did.[240]

240. Lerner, p. 36.

Bibliography

Alpenfalls, E. "Progressive Monogamy: An Alternative Pattern?" In Herbert A. Otto, ed., *The Family in Search of a Future* (New York: Appleton-Century-Crofts, 1970), pp. 67–74.

Ariés, Philippe. *Centuries of Childhood*. New York: Random House, Inc., 1962.

Bartz, Karen W., and F. Ivan Nye. "Early Marriage: A Propositional Formulation." *Journal of Marriage and the Family*, 32 (May, 1970), 258–68.

Baumann, K. E. "The Relationship Between Age at First Marriage, School Dropout, and Marital Instability: An Analysis of the Glick Effect." *Journal of Marriage and the Family*, 29 (November, 1967), 672–80.

Beal, Frances M. "Double Jeopardy: To Be Black and Female." In Robin Morgan, ed., *Sisterhood Is Powerful* (New York: Random House, Inc., 1970), pp. 340–52.

Beard, Mary R. *Woman as a Force in History*. New York: The Macmillan Company, 1946.

Bell, Daniel. "The Year 2,000—The Trajectory of an Idea." *Daedalus* 96 (Summer, 1967), 639–51.

Ben-Yosef, A. C. *The Purest Democracy in the World*. New York: Herzl Press, 1963.

Berger, Bennett, et al. "Child-Rearing Practices of the Communal Family." In Skolnick and Skolnick, eds., *Family in Transition* (Boston: Little, Brown and Company, 1971), pp. 509–22.

Berger, Peter L., and Brigette Berger. "The Blueing of America." *The New Republic* (April 3, 1971), 20–23.

Bernard, J. *Academic Women*. University Park, Pa.: Pennsylvania State University Press, 1964.

———. "The Adjustments of Married Mates." In H. T. Christensen, ed., *Handbook of Marriage and the Family* (Chicago: Rand McNally & Co., 1964), pp. 675–739.

———. "Women, Marriage, and the Future." *The Futurist*, 4 (April, 1970), 41–43.

Billingsley, A. *Black Families in White America*. Englewood Cliffs, N.J.: Prentice-Hall, Inc., 1968.

Bird, Caroline. *Born Female*. New York: David McKay Co., Inc., 1968.

Blau, Peter M. *Exchange and Power in Social Life.* New York: John Wiley & Sons, Inc., 1964.

Blood, R. O., Jr., and D. M. Wolfe. *Husbands and Wives.* New York: The Free Press, 1960.

Bockley, Walter. *Sociology and Modern Systems Theory.* Englewood Cliffs, N.J.: Prentice-Hall, Inc., 1967.

Bohannan, Paul, ed. *Divorce and After.* New York: Doubleday & Company, Inc., 1970.

Bronfenbrenner, Urie. "The Changing Soviet Family." In D. R. Brown, ed., *The Role and Status of Women in the Soviet Union* (New York: Teachers College Press, 1968), pp. 98–124.

Brown, Judith B. "Female Liberation First, and Now." In Roszak and Roszak, eds., *Masculine-Feminine: Readings in Sexual Mythology and the Liberation of Women* (New York: Harper & Row, Publishers, 1969), pp. 222–29.

Calverton, W. F. *The Bankruptcy of Marriage.* New York: The Macaulay Co., 1928.

Carcopino, Jerome. *Daily Life in Ancient Rome.* New Haven: Yale University Press, 1940.

Carter, Hugh, and Paul C. Glick. *Marriage and Divorce: A Social and Economic Study.* Cambridge, Mass.: Harvard University Press, 1970.

"Church Commune: A Shared Concern." *Chicago Daily News* (March 22, 1971).

Clarkson, F. E., et al. "Family Size and Sex Role Stereo Types." *Science* (January, 1970), 390–92.

Clignet, Remi. *Many Wives, Many Powers.* Evanston, Ill.: Northwestern University Press, 1970.

Constantine, L., and J. Constantine. "Where is Marriage Going?" *The Futurist,* 4 (April, 1970), 44–46.

Coombs, Lolagene, R. Freedman, and W. F. Pratt. "Premarital Pregnancy and Status Before and After Marriage." *American Journal of Sociology,* 75 (March, 1970), 800–820.

Coser, Lewis A. *The Functions of Social Conflict.* New York: The Free Press, 1956.

———. *Continuities in the Study of Social Conflict.* New York: The Free Press, 1967.

Cutright, Phillips. "Income and Family Events: Marital Stability." *Journal of Marriage and the Family,* 33 (May, 1971), 291–308.

Dahlström, Edmund, ed. *The Changing Roles of Men and Women.* London: G. Duckworth & Co., 1967.

D'Andrade, Roy G. "Sex Differences and Cultural Institutions." In E. E. Maccoby, ed., *The Development of Sex Differences* (Stanford, Calif.: Stanford University Press, 1966), pp. 173–203.

Davidson, Sara. "The Hippie Alternative: Getting Back to the Communal Garden." In Skolnick and Skolnick, eds., *Family in Transition* (Boston: Little, Brown and Company, 1971), pp. 523–42.

Degler, C. N. "Revolution Without Ideology: The Changing Place of Women in America." In R. J. Lifton, ed., *The Woman in America* (Boston: Beacon Press, 1964), pp. 193–210.

Denfeld, D., and M. Gordon. "Mate Swapping: The Family that Swings Together Clings Together." In Skolnick and Skolnick, eds., *Family in Transition* (Boston: Little, Brown and Company, 1971), pp. 463–75.

Divorce in California: 1966. State of California, Dept. of Public Health, Bureau of Vital Statistics, Sacramento (October, 1967).

Dodge, N. D. *Women in the Soviet Economy.* Baltimore: Johns Hopkins Press, 1966.

Downing, Joseph J. "The Tribal Family and the Society of Awakening." In Herbert A. Otto, ed., *The Family in Search of a Future* (New York: Appleton-Century-Crofts, 1970), pp. 119–36.

Dunbar, Roxanne. "Female Liberation as the Basis for Social Revolution." In Robin Morgan, ed., *Sisterhood Is Powerful* (New York: Random House, Inc., 1970), pp. 477–94.

Durham, M. "The Happy Hemmaman." *Life* (August 15, 1969), 46–47.

Ellis, Albert. "Group Marriage: A Possible Alternative." In Herbert A. Otto, ed., *The Family in Search of a Future* (New York: Appleton-Century-Crofts, 1970), pp. 85–98.

Engels, Frederick. "The Transformation of the Family." In N. W. Bell and E. F. Vogel, eds., *A Modern Introduction To the Family* (New York: The Free Press, 1968), pp. 45–47.

Farber, Bernard. *Family: Organization and Interaction.* San Francisco: Chandler Publishing Co., 1964.

Farley, Jennie. "Graduate Women: Career Aspirations and Family Size." *American Psychologist,* 25 (December, 1970), 1099–1100.

Farson, R. E.; P. M. Hauser, H. Stroup, and A. J. Wiener. *The Future of the Family.* New York: Family Service Association of America, 1969.

Field, Mark G. "Workers (and Mothers): Soviet Women Today." In D. R. Brown, ed., *The Role and Status of Women in the Soviet Union* (New York: Teachers College Press, 1968), pp. 7–56.

Figes, Eva. *Patriarchal Attitudes: Women in Society.* London: Faber & Faber, Ltd., 1970.

Ford, C. S. "Some Primitive Societies." In G. H. Seward and R. C. Williamson, eds., *Sex Roles in Changing Society* (New York: Random House, Inc., 1970), pp. 25–43.

Furstenberg, Frank F., Jr. "Industrialization and the American Family: A Look Backward." *American Sociological Review,* 31 (June, 1966), 326–37.

Geiger, H. Kent. *The Family in Soviet Russia.* Cambridge: Harvard University Press, 1968.

Gendell, Murray. *Swedish Working Wives.* Totowa, N.J.: The Bedminister Press, 1963.

Glick, P. C. and A. J. Norton. "Frequency, Duration, and Probability of Marriage and Divorce." *Journal of Marriage and Family,* 33 (May, 1971), 307–17.

Goode, William J. *After Divorce.* New York: The Free Press, 1956.

―――――. "The Theoretical Importance of Love." *American Sociological Review,* 24 (February, 1959), 38–47.

―――――. *World Revolution and Family Patterns.* New York: The Free Press, 1963.

―――――. "Family Disorganization." In R. K. Merton and R. A. Nisbet, eds., *Contemporary Social Problems* (New York: Harcourt Brace Jovanovich, 1966), pp. 479–552.

―――――. "Marital Satisfaction and Instability: A Cross-Cultural, Class Analysis of Divorce Rates." In R. Bendix and S. M. Lipset, eds., *Class, Status, and Power* (New York: The Free Press, 1966), pp. 377–87.

―――――. "The Theory and Measurement of Family Change." In E. B. Sheldon and W. E. Moore, eds., *Indicators of Social Change* (New York: Russel Sage, 1968), pp. 295–348.

―――――, ed. *Readings on the Family and Society.* Englewood Cliffs, N.J.: Prentice-Hall, Inc., 1964.

Gordon, M., and M. C. Bernstein. "Mate Choice and Domestic Life in the Nineteenth-Century Marriage Manual." *Journal of Marriage and Family,* 32 (November, 1970), 665–74.

Gouldner, A. W. "The Norm of Reciprocity: A Preliminary Statement." *American Sociological Review,* 25 (April, 1960), 161–78.

Grønseth, Erik. "The Dysfunctionality of the Husband Provider Role in Industrialized Societies." Paper read at the Seventh World Congress of Sociology, 1970, Varna, Bulgaria.

Groves, E. R., and W. F. Ogburn. *American Marriage and Family Relationships.* New York: Holt & Co., 1928.

Hicks, M. W., and P. Platt. "Marital Happiness and Stability: A Review of the Research in the Sixties." *Journal of Marriage and the Family,* 32 (November, 1970), 553–74.

Hobart, C. W. "Commitment, Value Conflict, and the Future of the American Family." *Marriage and Family Living,* 25 (November, 1963), 405–11.

Hoffman, Lois W. "Parental Power Relations and the Division of Household Tasks." *Marriage and Family Living,* 22 (February, 1960), 27–35.

————, and F. Wyatt. "Social Change and Motivations for Having Larger Families: Some Theoretical Considerations." *Merrill-Palmer Quarterly,* 6 (1960), 235–44.

Holter, Harriet. *Sex Roles and Social Structure.* Oslo: Universitetsforlarget, 1970.

Horner, Matina S. "Femininity and Successful Achievement: A Basic Inconsistency." In J. M. Bardwick, et al., *Feminine Personality and Conflict* (Belmont, Calif.: Brooks/ Cole Pub. Co., 1970), pp. 45–76.

Hunt, C. L. "Female Occupational Roles and Urban Sex Ratios in the United States, Japan, and the Philippines." *Social Forces,* Vol. 43 (March, 1965), pp. 407–17.

Johnson, Ralph. "Some Correlates of Extramarital Coitus." *Journal of Marriage and the Family,* 32 (August, 1970), 449–56.

Jones, Beverly. "Radical Women as Students." In Roszak and Roszak, eds., *Masculine-Feminine: Readings in Sexual Mythology and the Liberation of Women* (New York: Harper & Row, Publishers 1969), pp. 213–22.

Kaberry, Phyllis M. *Women of the Grassfields.* London: Her Majesty's Stationery Office, 1953.

Kaley, M. M. "Attitudes Toward the Dual Role of the Married Professional Woman." *American Psychologist,* 26 (March, 1971), 301–6.

Kelman, Steven. "Sweden's Liberated Men and Women." *The New Republic* (March 13, 1971), pp. 21–23.

King, H. H. "The Black Woman and Womens Lib." *Ebony* (March, 1971), pp. 68–76.

Komarovsky, Mirra. *Women in the Modern World: Their Education and Their Dilemmas.* Boston: Little, Brown & Company, 1953.

————. *Blue-Collar Marriage.* New York: Random House, Inc., 1962.

Kraditor, Aileen S. *Up from the Pedestal.* Chicago: Quadrangle Books, 1968.

La Rue, Linda J. M., "Black Liberation and Women's Lib." *Trans Action,* 8 (November–December, 1970), 59–64.

Lauriat, Patience. "The Effect of Marital Dissolution on Fertility." *Journal of Marriage and Family,* 31 (August, 1969), 484–93.

Lebergott, Stanley. "Population Change and the Supply of Labor." In *Demographic and Economic Change in Developed Countries* (Princeton, N.J.: Princeton University Press, 1960), pp. 370–90.

Leon, Dan. *The Kibbutz.* Tel Aviv: Israel Horizons Publisher, 1964.

Lerner, Max. *Los Angeles Times Syndicate.* June, 1971.

Liljeström, Rita. "The Swedish Model." In G. H. Seward and R. C. Williamson, eds., *Sex Roles in Changing Society* (New York: Random House, Inc., 1970), pp. 200–219.

Linn, E. L. "Women Dentists: Career and Family." *Social Problems,* 18 (Winter, 1971), 393–403.

Lupri, Eugen. "Contemporary Authority Patterns in the West German Family: A Study in Cross-National Validation." *Journal of Marriage and Family,* 31 (February, 1969), 34–44.

McCall, Michal M. "Courtship as Social Exchange." In Bernard Farber, ed., *Kinship and Family Organization* (New York: John Wiley & Sons, Inc., 1966), pp. 190–210.

McKinley, D. G. *Social Class and Family Life.* New York: The Free Press, 1964.

Mead, Margaret. "The Life Cycle and Its Variations: The Division of Roles." *Daedalus,* 96 (Summer, 1967), 871–75.

———. "Marriage in Two Steps." In Herbert A. Otto, ed., *The Family in Search of a Future* (New York: Appleton-Century-Crofts, 1970), pp. 75–84.

Mill, John Stuart. *The Subjection of Women and Other Essays.* London: Oxford University Press, 1869.

Miller, S. M., and P. Roby. *The Future of Inequality.* New York: Basic Books, 1970.

Milton, John. "The Doctrine and Discipline of Divorce." In W. Petersen and D. Matza, eds., *Social Controversy* (Belmont, Calif.: Wadsworth, 1963), pp. 83–89.

Mitchell, Juliet. "The Longest Revolution." In Roszak and Roszak, eds., *Masculine-Feminine: Readings in Sexual Mythology and the Liberation of Women* (New York: Harper & Row, Publishers, 1969), pp. 160–73.

Mizruchi, E. *Success and Opportunity.* New York: The Free Press, 1964.

Mogey, J. M. "A Century of Declining Paternal Authority." *Marriage and Family Living,* 19 (August, 1957), 234–39.

Morgan, Robin. "Goodbye To All That." In Roszak and Roszak, eds., *Masculine-Feminine* (New York: Harper & Row, Publishers, 1969), pp. 241–48.

———, ed. *Sisterhood Is Powerful.* New York: Random House, Inc., 1970.

Murdock, George P. *Social Structure.* New York: The Macmillan Company, 1949.

Murray, Pauli. "The Liberation of Black Women." In Mary Lou Thompson, ed., *Voices of the New Feminism* (Boston: Beacon Press, 1970), pp. 87–102.

Neubeck, Gerhard. *Extramarital Relations.* Englewood Cliffs, N.J.: Prentice-Hall, Inc., 1969.

———. "Polyandry and Polygyny: Viable Today?" In Herbert A. Otto, ed., *The Family in Search of a Future* (New York: Appleton-Century-Crofts, 1970), pp. 99–110.

Norton, E. H. "For Sadie and Maude." In Morgan, ed., *Sisterhood Is Powerful* (New York: Random House, Inc., 1970), pp. 353–59.

Nye, F. Ivan. "Values, Family, and a Changing Society." *Journal of Marriage and the Family,* 29 (May, 1967), 241–48.

———, et al. "A Partial Theory of Marital Dissolution." Unpublished paper. Pullman: Washington State University, 1968.

O'Neill, W. L. *Divorce in the Progressive Era.* New Haven: Yale University Press, 1967.

———. *The Woman Movement: Feminism in the United States and England.* New York: Barnes & Noble, Inc., 1969.

Oppenheimer, Valerie K. "Demographic Influences on Female Employment and the Status of Women." Paper read at the meetings of the American Association for the Advancement of Science, December, 1970.

Orleans, M., and F. Wolfson. "The Future of the Family." *The Futurist,* 4 (April, 1970), 48–49.

Otto, Herbert A., ed. *The Family in Search of a Future.* New York: Appleton-Century-Crofts, 1970.

Parke, R. J., and P. C. Glick. "Prospective Changes in Marriage and the Family." *Journal of Marriage and the Family,* 29 (May, 1967), 249–56.

Paulme, Denise, ed. *Women of Tropical Africa.* Berkeley: University of California Press, 1963.

Piercy, Marge. "The Grand Coolie Damn." In Morgan, ed., *Sisterhood Is Powerful* (New York: Random House, Inc., 1970), pp. 438–46.

Plateris, Alexander A. *Divorce Statistics Analysis, United States, 1963.* U.S. Public Health Service, Series 21, No. 13, October, 1967.

―――. *Divorce Statistics Analysis, United States, 1964 and 1965.* U.S. Public Health Service, Series 21, No. 17, October, 1969.

―――. *Children of Divorced Couples: United States, Selected Years.* U.S. Public Health Service, Series 21, No. 18, February, 1970.

―――. *Increases In Divorces, United States, 1967.* U.S. Public Health Service, Series 21, No. 20, December, 1970.

Rabin, A. I. "The Sexes: Ideology and Reality in the Israeli Kibbutz." In G. H. Seward and R. C. Williamson, eds., *Sex Roles in Changing Society* (New York: Random House, Inc., 1970), pp. 285–307.

Rainwater, Lee. *Family Design.* Chicago: Aldine Press, 1965.

―――. "Crucible of Identity: The Negro Lower-Class Family." *Daedalus,* 95 (Winter, 1966), 172–216.

Renne, Karen S. "Correlates of Dissatisfaction in Marriage." *Journal of Marriage and the Family,* 32 (February, 1970), 54–67.

Rossi, Alice S. "The Road to Sex Equality." Unpublished paper. Baltimore: Goucher College, 1969.

―――. "Deviance and Conformity in the Life Goals of Women." Unpublished paper. Baltimore: Goucher College, 1970.

Roszak, Betty, and T. Roszak, eds. *Masculine-Feminine: Readings in Sexual Mythology and the Liberation of Women.* New York: Harper & Row, Publishers, 1969.

Ruderman, F. A. *Child Care and Working Mothers.* New York: Child Welfare League of America, 1968.

Sandlund, MajBritt. *The Status of Women in Sweden.* Report to the United Nations, 1968. Stockholm: The Swedish Institute.

Satir, Virginia. "Marriage as a Human-Actualizing Contract." In Herbert A. Otto, ed., *The Family in Search of a Future* (New York: Appleton-Century-Crofts, 1970), pp. 57–66.

Scanzoni, John. "A Social System Analysis of Dissolved and Existing Marriages." *Journal of Marriage and the Family,* 30 (August, 1968), 452–61.

―――. *Opportunity and the Family.* New York: The Free Press, 1970.

―――. *The Black Family in Modern Society.* Boston: Allyn and Bacon, Inc., 1971.

Schor, Alvin L. "The Family Cycle and Income Development." In Louis A. Ferman, et al., eds., *Poverty in America* (Ann Arbor: University of Michigan Press, 1968), pp. 39–61.

Sears, Robert R. "Development of Gender Role." In Frank A. Beach, ed., *Sex and Behavior* (New York: John Wiley & Sons, Inc., 1965), pp. 133–63.

Shepher, J. "Familism and Social Structure: The Case of the Kibbutz." *Journal of Marriage and Family*, 31 (August, 1969), 567–73.

Skolnick, A. S., and J. H. Skolnick, eds. *Family in Transition*. Boston: Little, Brown and Company, 1971.

Smuts, R. W. *Women and Work in America*. New York: Columbia University Press, 1959.

Southall, Aiden, ed. *Social Change in Modern Africa*. New York: Oxford University Press, 1961.

Speigel, John P. "The Resolution of Role Conflict Within the Family." In N. W. Bell and E. F. Vogel, eds, *A Modern Introduction to the Family* (New York: The Free Press, 1968), pp. 391–411.

Spiro, M. *Kibbutz: Venture in Utopia*. Cambridge, Mass.: Harvard University Press, 1956.

———. *Children of the Kibbutz*. Cambridge, Mass.: Harvard University Press, 1958.

———. "Is the Family Universal? The Israeli Case." In N. W. Bell and E. F. Vogel, eds., *A Modern Introduction to the Family* (New York: The Free Press, 1968), pp. 68–79.

Sprey, Jetse. "The Family as a System in Conflict." *Journal of Marriage and the Family*, 31 (November, 1969), 699–706.

"Statement on Birth Control." In Robin Morgan, ed., *Sisterhood Is Powerful* (New York: Random House, Inc., 1970), pp. 360–61.

Steinmann, Anne, Fox, D. J., and R. Farkas. "Male and Female Perceptions of Male Sex Roles." *Proceedings of the American Psychological Association* (1968), pp. 421–22.

Stoller, F. H. "The Intimate Network of Families as a New Structure." In Herbert A. Otto, ed., *The Family in Search of a Future* (New York: Appleton-Century-Crofts, 1970), pp. 145–60.

Stryker, Sheldon. "Role-Taking: Accuracy and Adjustment." *Sociometry*, 20 (1957), 127–33.

Sussman, Marvin B. "Theoretical Bases for an Urban Kinship Network System." Unpublished paper. Cleveland: Case-Western Reserve University, 1966.

Turner, Ralph H. *Family Interaction*. New York: John Wiley & Sons, Inc., 1970.

Tyler, A. F. *Freedom's Ferment*. New York: Harper & Row, Publishers, 1944.

Udry, J. Richard. "Marital Instability by Race, Sex, Education, and Occupation, Using 1960 Census Data." *American Journal of Sociology*, 72 (September, 1966), 203–9.

Walshok, Mary L. "The Social Correlates and Sexual Consequences of Variations in Gender Role Orientation. A National Study of College Students." Unpublished dissertation. Bloomington: Indiana University, 1969.

Westley, A. W., and N. B. Epstein. *Silent Majority*. San Francisco: Jossey-Boss, Inc., 1969.

Wilensky, Harold L. "Work as a Social Problem." In H. S. Becker, ed., *Social Problems: A Modern Approach* (New York: John Wiley & Sons, Inc., 1966), pp. 117–66.

Winch, Robert F. *The Modern Family*. New York: Holt, Rinehart & Winston, 1963, 1971.

Yette, Samuel, *Newsweek Feature Service* (June 27, 1971).

Zelditch, Morris, Jr. "Family, Marriage, and Kinship." In R. E. L. Faris, ed., *Handbook of Modern Sociology* (Chicago: Rand McNally & Co. 1964), pp. 362–95.

U.S. Bureau of the Census. *Current Population Reports.* Series P–20, No. 212 (February 1, 1971).

————. *Current Population Reports.* Series P–23, Special Studies, No. 27 (1969).

————. *Current Population Reports.* Series P–20, No. 187 (August 11, 1969).

————. *Current Population Reports.* Series P–20, No. 198 (March 25, 1970).

————. *Current Population Reports.* Series P–23, No. 36 (April 16, 1971).

————. *Current Population Reports.* Series P–23, No. 32 (July 29, 1970).

————. *Current Population Reports.* Series P–60, No. 64 (October 6, 1969).

————. *Current Population Reports.* "School Enrollment: October, 19, 1970." Series P–20, No. 222 (June 28, 1971).

————. *Current Population Reports,* Series P–20, No. 223 (October 7, 1971).

————. *Current Population Reports, Series* P–20, No. 225 (November, 1971).

U.S. Public Health Service. *Monthly Vital Statistics Report* (National Natality Survey Statistics), Vol. 18, No. 12, Supplement (March 27, 1970).

INDEX

Index

Divorce *(cont.)*
  refined, 8–9
Divorce (variations in)
  by age, 16–18, 20–21
  cross-national comparisons, 14–16
  by education, 18–19
  by husband's occupation, 19
  by income, 19
  by race, 23–25
Dodge, N., 113, 133
Downing, J., 9, 104, 110
Dunbar, R., 5
Durham, M., 152
Duties, ratio to right, in marriage, 36 ff.

Education, divorce variations by, 18–19
Ellis, A., 116, 122
Engels, F., 29
Employment of married women, 33, 40, 70, 108, 125, 129–33. *See also* Achievement, occupational, for women; Work
Epstein, N., 52
Equality. *See* Rights-duties ratio in marriage; Role; Sex and sex-role equality; Social exchange; Women; Women's Liberation
Evaluating in marital conflict, 89
Expressive dimension in marital roles, 36 ff., 63 ff., 142, 160–61
Extended family (blood and non-blood), 113–14, 157–58

Family
  Extended (blood and nonblood), 113–14, 157–58
  Intimate network, 114–15
  Patterns, black, 23–25, 70, 120, 156

Family *(cont.)*
  Structure
    cross-national comparisons in, 113, 126–36, 143 ff.
    consumption patterns, 158 ff.
    Soviet, 15, 133–36, 162
    Swedish, 131–32
Farber, 26
Farley, J., 152
Farson, 104, 120
Femininity as passivity, 48
Feminism (and neofeminism), 41–42, 81, 106, 129, 150. *See also* Women; Women's Liberation
Field, M., 40, 50, 134
Figes, E., 79, 93, 122–23, 127, 146, 160
Ford, C., 144
Freud, S., 48, 79, 94
Furstenberg, F., 35, 37
Future trends in divorce, 85, 139

Game theory, 31, 72
Geiger, K., 15, 20, 113, 134
Glick, P., 6, 11, 17–19, 23, 27, 57–59, 85, 139, 143
Goode, W. J., 10, 15, 20, 26, 31, 33, 40. 42, 101, 124, 148
Gordon, M., 34–116
Gouldner, A., 62
Grønseth, E., 144–45
Group marriage, 115
Groves, E., 7

Hicks, M., 26
Hobart, C., 54
Hoffman, L., 40, 161
Holter, H., 75, 145–47
Horner, M., 48, 150
Hostility, 78, 99–100. *See also* Conflict
Hunt, C., 108